THE GENTLE ART OF
SPIRITUAL GUIDANCE

THE GENTLE ART OF SPIRITUAL GUIDANCE

JOHN R. YUNGBLUT

CONTINUUM • NEW YORK

1995

The Continuum Publishing Company
370 Lexington Avenue
New York, NY 10017

Copyright © 1988 by John R. Yungblut

Printed in the United States of America

Library of Congress Cataloging-in-Publication Data

Yungblut, John R.
    The gentle art of spiritual guidance / John R. Yungblut.
        p.   cm.
    Includes bibliographical references.
    ISBN 0-8264-0750-1 (pbk. : alk. paper)
    1. Spiritual direction.   I. Title.
BV5053.Y86   1995
253.5'3'—dc20   95-33091
                                                             CIP

ACKNOWLEDGMENTS

Books often have their antecedents in early experiences and commitments of their authors. This one is no exception. How shall I express gratitude to those who have helped me with the process of preparing it for publication without recollecting the profound influence initially exerted upon my thinking by a handful of teachers and mentors who, as I see them now, were among my first spiritual guides. The tap roots of my approach to the art of spiritual guidance lie in the impact on my mind of certain figures during my undergraduate days at Harvard University.

Rufus Jones was my favorite preacher. He came regularly to the college chapel. When I finally tracked down the source of the bouyance and joie de vive that made his countenance radiant, I was led to the nourishment his spirit had derived over the years from the apostolic succession of Christian mystics. When Alfred North Whitehead lectured, the expression on his face reflected what I concluded must be nothing less than beatific vision. With him, Philosophy was once again the handmaid of true religion. Kirtley Mather, descendant of the early American evangelist, Cotton Mather, one of the liveliest of lecturers because of his passionate interest in his subject, introduced me to the demonstrable fact of evolution while sharing his own unique synthesis of his scientific discipline and his Christian faith. Finally, Henry Cadbury at the Harvard Divinity School raised all the ultimate questions concerning Christology while steadfastly refusing to answer any of them for his students.

Later, as this book will abundantly testify, I came under the influence of Pierre Teilhard de Chardin and C. G. Jung. I have remained a student of both ever since. In my quest of my own personal myth of meaning, I have had to assimilate the fresh revelation arising from the fact of evolution and the accumulating wisdom of depth psychology. Teilhard's vision and Jung's psychology have enabled me to re-mythologize the traditional Christ myth with which I grew up. They helped me to win a viable faith of my own. My personal indebtedness to the mystical heritage and to the insights of these two prophets and apologists for religion will be apparent.

Now for acknowledgment of valuable help in the preparation of the manuscript. Jane O'Brien typed the first draft, a labor of love. Douglas Steere, in addition to favoring me with a preface, gave valuable suggestions regarding the presentation of material. Morton Kelsey, Pir Vilayat Inayat Khan, Mary Shaw May, and Mary Love May were good enough to read the manuscript and make useful critiques.

Members of the Guild for Spiritual Guidance of the last decade have entered into dialogue with me as I shared with them the convictions here presented, thereby bestowing on my preparation for writing this book greater authenticity through the sustained encounter.

Finally, I would express deep gratitude to my wife, Penelope, for probing questions, skillful editing, and unfailing encouragement.

CONTENTS

PREFACE

In every generation there have been a few explorers who were not content to ply their boats in the small well-charted paths of the downstream regions of great rivers. Instead they have chosen to go on upstream to get nearer to the source. If we get inside the contemporary scene in the religious life of Britain and America, it is heartening to find a few just such sensitive explorers who have in their own way headed upstream. They have done it in the hope not only of getting nearer to the Source themselves, but of learning how to guide others to that Source of renewal.

Some years ago Britain's Kenneth Leech, an Anglican, wrote a widely-read masterpiece called *Soul Friend* that traced the whole Christian history of spiritual guidance and direction. In Washington D.C., three years later, an Episcopal priest, Tilden Edwards, published a book, *Spiritual Friend*, in which he shares his own experience as a guide of souls. Now John Yungblut in this impressive book, *The Gentle Art of Spiritual Guidance*, has revealed his own concern as both an explorer and a seasoned guide in finding authentic ways to assist seeking persons to move on

upstream and to "Come in, come in, come still further in,"
to the Source.

This book is not a mere manual or a work-book, for
spiritual guidance is indeed not a formulatable science but
a "gentle art". Yet in his book there is a rich and moving
sharing not only of an intellectual frame in which a modern
mind can move and be inspired by its invitation to "come
still further in" but it carries many helpful suggestions to
prepare oneself to assist others in their interior journey.

John Yungblut quotes with approval the statement that
"a mystic is not a special kind of person but rather that every
person is a special kind of mystic." The heart of his
approach is that upstream Christian faith really begins when
I realize that I am infinitely loved by God who is with me
always. But it does not end there. Harry Williams carries
the further step in his words, "It is only to the degree in
which we begin to apprehend God's love for me that I can
begin to apprehend his love for all men. . .and that is the
main spring of all Christian social action."

John Yungblut has been an Episcopal minister who in
mid-life joined the Religious Society of Friends. He has since
that time been a Quaker presence in Atlanta, Washington
D.C., South Africa's Johannesburg, and has served as a
spiritual guide and teacher at Pendle Hill, a Quaker center
for religious and social studies. This book in its first four
chapters reflects his own inward journey and is an admirable
addition to his three previous books: *Rediscovering Prayer,
Rediscovering the Christ,* and *Discovering God Within.* In
that previous trilogy, as in this volume, Teilhard de Chardin
and C.G. Jung have helped him to rethink the mysteries of
the Christian religion and to see them converging in an
evolutionary and individuating frame that is at home with
science and with the best psychotherapeutic insights of our
time.

In the fifth chapter "Cultivating the Gift for Spiritual
Guidance," he moves on from his impressive description
of this frame that has both drawn and liberated him in his
own journey to the Source. From this point on he deals with
the delicate art of guiding other explorers in their quest to
respond more completely to the God within. This chapter

is based upon John's ten year experience as Director of the Guild for Spiritual Guidance that is located among the other offerings of Wainwright House in Rye, New York, where participants — known as apprentices — are taken through a two year experience in which the nurture of the interior life is explored.

This program, a program which continues to grow in strength as it is repeated, was built around John Yungblut's leadership and owes much of its amazing power of inner deepening to his close, personal, and gentle conferring with each member. To this was added his gift for holding together this remarkable company of guest-teachers of all species with Episcopalians, Roman Catholics, Russian Orthodox, Presbyterians and Quakers among them. He also encouraged the close togetherness of groups of twos and fours among each Guild group whose intimacy in sharing and conferring gave more than a glimpse of what would be asked of them in their later practice of spiritual guidance in whatever circumstances it might occur.

The sixth chapter of the book sparkles with his delightful sharing of his own favorite books of spiritual reading. Keenly aware that, as Baron von Hügel says, "No two souls are ever dittos", his seventh chapter is full of priceless wisdom that has come out of his decades of experience as well as out of his own pilgrimage. The eighth and final chapter interprets the personal transformation by which the author of the Fourth Gospel became and remains one of the great spiritual guides of all time.

In these post-Vatican days when the walls between the varied Christian denominations have been crumbling, it is exciting to see these daring explorers within the non-Roman Catholic World rediscovering this ancient practice of the guidance of souls and daring to reframe and to refashion it to meet the hunger of our time. In this book John Yungblut has carried this fresh discovery another long mile on its journey.

Douglas V. Steere
Haverford College

For Penelope, my beloved wife, in dialogue with whom this book took its final form.

INTRODUCTION

In writing this book, I am addressing primarily that solitary individual who has already recognized a stirring or prompting within his or her heart that has evoked a sense of possible vocation for the awesome work of spiritual guidance. I would help that person in further discernment of this gift, this ministry, for which the ordination is from on high. I would also speak to the seeker who has sincerely and consciously embarked on the inward journey to the self and is therefore aware of the need for a spiritual guide. For the journey to the self is at the same time the great journey to the Self, the God who dwells within.

At the tercentenary celebration of the founding of Harvard College, one of the citations accompanying the conferring of an honorary degree referred to psychology as "the newest of the sciences, the oldest of the arts". I shall insist that spiritual guidance as practiced in the twentieth century must take into account the accumulating insights of modern depth psychology, especially those emerging from Carl Jung's myth of the psyche. It must also be in harmony with the laws operative in the universe as revealed

1

by the natural sciences in the twentieth century. I shall argue that contemporary spiritual guidance must be placed in the context of continuing creation through evolution as discerned by Teilhard de Chardin in his myth of cosmogenesis (a cosmos still being born).

Yet, although it must include and draw upon the findings of the natural sciences, spiritual guidance is not itself a science. It is an art and can lay claim to already having been in practice as man and woman emerged into consciousness from their animal forebears through the mysterious and wonderful power of reflection. Some men and women were endowed with gifts that enabled them to sense with assurance the direction that pointed to still higher consciousness. They responded affirmatively to these insights and knew instinctively how to quicken a like motivation in others. This involved the practice of an art, far from a conscious art as yet, but nevertheless an art: the art of spiritual guidance. Even before words "were", in the sense of a versatile language, this inner Word was heard and responded to by some. I will make bold to claim for it that spiritual guidance is not only the oldest but also the greatest of the arts because it has to do with what it means to keep on transcending oneself in the process, not yet plumbed, of becoming human.

This art grows ever more subtle and complex as consciousness keeps rising. At its core, however, it has to do with a great and ultimate simplicity: helping the human psyche realize its inherent destiny, its still unrealized potential within the vast ongoing process of evolution, to find its way home to its own center, God, through a kind of unfolding incarnation. Before the revelation of the fact of evolution, spiritual guidance within the Christian phylum could be represented as a means of helping individuals through their tortuous course in this "vale of tears" to the distant shore of another world. This world was at best a precarious opportunity to win passage to this other world, a happier place beyond, through faithfulness to a code of conduct and commitment to a set of beliefs. Now this art must be conceived as practiced within a totally different context, a different perception of the very meaning and purpose of life, of where life is coming from on this earth and where it is tending, of what can be discerned about the as-yet-unlived life whose seed lies deep within the human psyche awaiting liberation and incarnation within the fullness of time.

A new sense of the portentousness of spiritual guidance begins to dawn upon us. I think of the dark but promising and pregnant atmosphere that pervades the background of some of Rouault's paintings. The very form and color of the sky, cloud, sun, or moon project a mystical sense that the whole cosmos is somehow involved in what is happening here, now, at this moment. In one of Rouault's paintings, "The Sea of Galilee", Jesus seems to be calling James and John away from their parents and wives and fishing nets to be "fishers of men". The present moment is endowed with cosmic significance because it transcends itself and radiates the promise of a glory that only the future can reveal. It is a beginning, a "birthing", of universal import.

This book will attempt to interpret spiritual guidance as no less than the art of discerning "that of God" in another and helping that individual be true to this divine spark, not in some vague aspiration, which in any case must have its compensatory counterpart in the form of a lurking shadow (as we shall see), but by way of implementation in hard moral choices, in detachment from "inordinate desires and affections", in "right ordering" of relationships and proper use of talents, etc. In this newly perceived context spiritual guidance is a matter of being an instrument by which the divine course can find its way in this other solitary individual so that the crucial inward journey of this child of God may become creatively aligned with the immense journey of evolution itself, moving through the human species to the unknown ultimate destination of fully raised consciousness. We do not and cannot see the distant scene. One step is enough for us: a step in the direction of Christ-consciousness, individuation, wholeness.

Something much greater than individual salvation is involved. The woman or man who has the courage and stamina to embark on this inward journey and to assist another in keeping on course becomes, to a degree Paul never dreamed, a co-creater with God, not only within the confines of her or his own life, but also on behalf of a still-evolving species and a process as vast as a cosmos still being born. At the same time if she or he yields to the prompting of the Spirit, despite the very considerable psychic dangers and besetting temptations involved (which we shall later explore), there will be a sense of being buoyed up, supported, by the vast groundswell of a current as old as time and as irresistible. It is a sense not only of my "going my way" but of my "going God's way" and therefore of the rightness of "letting go" and "letting be" in obedience to this totally reliable wisdom built into the structure of things.

We shall not downplay the lurking shadow of inflation for one who pursues this vocation. But should one fail to respond to the divine calling in order to avoid the risks involved? Obviously, one is to embark on this mission in fear and trembling, if authentically discerned by one's self and others. To deny the call, however, or to remain paralyzed between inaction and response, is to be disobedient in the worst way: to miss the one great chance to become and remain one's self in the service of God. Rather, one must obey the still small voice that persistently whispers, "For this was I born." While remaining intensely alert to all the shadow manifestations brought into play by this intolerably heavy persona, one is to commit one's self into God's keeping, knowing that appropriate humility will flow only from sustained consciousness of the love of God, to which the very first intimation of calling was already a response.

I have emphatically designated this supreme art as a "gentle" art. And gentle it is! This does not mean it is without firmness, and that strong "direction" is not indicated as an appropriate form of guidance under certain circumstances. I am referring to the inward posture of the guide. A figurative whack over the head when the individual appears drowsy or lethargic or an enforced *satori* through a mind-boggling *koan* (Buddhist style) may be applied, with humor, once in a long while. But the only sound, sustained milieu is one of gentleness because what is involved is a "tendering" process. The guide submits to becoming a channel through which the Spirit of God woos the wayward soul of this particular individual.

In one of the Psalms of David, repeated also in the Second Book of Samuel, all the more arresting because they follow a paean of praise of military virtues, are the unexpected and incongruous words, addressed to God, "Thy gentleness hath made me great" (Ps. 18:35). What a superb insight, whether it can be authentically attributed to David the King or not, Poetically it rings true. It faithfully identifies David's best gift, gentleness, quickened and evoked by the gentleness of God's love. In this passage, we may see the heart of David's mystical experience of the love of God. We do not condone David's aberrations and violations of the moral law. But the elements of greatness in him surely spring from this inherent strain of gentleness: the shepherd boy who first directed this gift toward the care of his sheep; the young man deeply moved by the quality of his own love for Jonathan; the healing gift that brought solace through gentle strains of music to the inflamed mind of Saul the King; the father overcome with grief for his lost son, Absalom. It is as if David recognized the source of his real strength: "Thy gentleness hath made me great." Those ministered to by David could have borne like testimony to him. And the end of that cycle, one suspects, is not yet, in the mysterious providence of God. One intuitively knows that this must inevitably be the unspoken but heartfelt tribute of every one who has ever been effectively ministered to by a genuine spiritual guide: "Thy gentleness hath made me great."

I shall endeavor to communicate what I have to say in this book as simply and as directly as I can because of the intensely personal and urgent nature of the material. I shall want to advocate a sense of unbroken continuity with the heritage of Christian spiritual direction or guidance, albeit updated, informed and reformed by certain insights of Jungian depth psychology, and as a historic process now perceived in the light of and with reference to our new comprehension of continuing creation through evolution as presented in Teilhard's myth of cosmogenesis. Attention will be given to the relationship between sexuality and spirituality. Some consideration will be given to the distinction between contemporary psychotherapy and spiritual guidance, and some directions for training for the vocation of spiritual guidance will be offered. There will be some suggestions for the cultivation of the contemplative faculty in the life of the guide and some reflections on the dynamics of the relationship between the guide and counselee in the one-to-one counseling session. Finally, I want to present the author of the Fourth Gospel and the Epistles of John as a spiritual guide par excellence.

CHAPTER 1

THE TRADITION OF CHRISTIAN SPIRITUAL GUIDANCE

Before the advent of the ~~Christian phylum~~ in the evolutionary ascent of the human species, forms of spiritual guidance already existed. Communities and societies of course developed mores and ritualistic practices. But there were individual persons, shamans or medicine men and women, who stood apart from the systems of direct authority, and exercised what can only be perceived from our perspective as a form of spiritual guidance. Persuaded by their own mystical experience of their divine calling, they did not hesitate to exert an enormous influence on the lives of others through a process which Jung would have called "unconscious prestige", a psychological leverage of which they themselves were unaware. We are referring to a form of communication, largely from unconscious to unconscious.

PRE-CHRISTIAN GUIDANCE

"Medicine man" is not an altogether good name for the practitioner of this art. "Shaman" is better because its connotations are more inclusive. It is true that part of the ministry involved altering physical conditions, healing the body. Herbs, plants, and roots of medicinal value were used. But many psychological factors were also at play. In addition, there was the numinous element to which we can refer as spiritual since it is the bond which interrelates all the other factors and makes not only for wholeness and therefore health of body, mind, and spirit, but also orients the solitary psyche with the very direction which evolution has developed and wants further to pursue. We shall explore the implications of all this later on. It is sufficient here to point out that Christian spiritual direction does not arise *de novo* with the advent of the Christian phylum among the living religions, but has its roots deep in the dynamics of the human psyche and in the continuing process of evolution.

This art, then, as old as the dawn of reflection, takes a distinctive and recognizable form with the Christian phylum, or more accurately within the Judaeo-Christian phylum, since there is an unbroken continuity in the development of Christianity from Judaeism. There are fine examples of spiritual guidance in the Old Testament. One thinks of the stature of that great shaman, Moses, and of his legacy to the children of Israel through the Ten Commandments; of Elijah and his message; of the direct calling of Samuel; of Nathan's charge to David the King. One thinks of Jeremiah's internalization of the Ten Commandments through his perception that God's laws, far from needing tablets of stone for inscription had been written on our inward parts, and of the great sharing of the Psalmists of their inward journey and their practice of "meditating on the laws of God day and night".

JESUS AS SPIRITUAL GUIDE

For my part I must assume that Jesus was fully human, more highly "hominized" than other men and women to be sure, but fully human. Seen from the evolutionary perspective, he could be called Christ the Evolver (as Teilhard de Chardin designated him) or Christ the fully individuated human being (as Jung saw him). Being human, as well as "the Second Adam", the Son of Man, he would have needed spiritual guidance as a child and growing young man. How did he rise to become the supreme spiritual guide of a large part of the human species? Who were *his* guides?

guides for Christ

A response to this involves what has been called the "scandal of particularity". Ogden Nash expressed it in the doggerel, "How odd of God to choose the Jews!" Of course, there is no scandal from an evolutionary point of view. Mutations leading to a new species have always come about through particular individuals in particular places at particular times. The breakthrough always awaits the coming of what paleontologists call the "sport", the more highly evolved individual of the species.

The truth is simply that at that particular moment and place in the larger panoply or fullness of time and space, the Jews alone among the peoples of the earth had created and preserved the songs, the stories, the prayers that could nourish the childhood and young manhood of one who was to become Jesus of Nazareth. They alone had in readiness the competent spiritual guides. We know that as a child Jesus frequented the Temple and conversed with elders and rabbis, precocious in his insight and understanding. His mother Mary was the favored one in whom the Holy Spirit conceived the Christ life, mystically, before she gave birth to the one who was to incarnate it. Whatever beatification may be bestowed upon Mary by a grateful church, is any other commendation needed beyond the obvious fact that she served the growing Jesus as his primary spiritual guide? And is any further commendation needed for Joseph beyond the fact that when Jesus sought to address God in the most natural, forthcoming way, he did not hesitate to say, as a child, "Abba, Father"? As Jesus grew older he may have spent some time with a monastic order known as the Essenes, in which he would have experienced more formal spiritual guidance by the equivalent of a novice master in a contemporary monastery.

We shall maintain that the call to serve as a spiritual guide in the Christian heritage always begins with the experience of being loved by God. "We love because he first loved us" (I John 4:19). In this the Master was not above the disciples. The prelude is always a mystical experience, or series of experiences, in which one is visited by the great Presence. Once reassured of being fully accepted and loved unconditionally, without reservations, one responds in love. For Jesus, whatever the antecedents, this took place at the time of his baptism, when he heard the voice of God proclaiming, "This is my beloved son, in whom I am well pleased" (Matt. 3:17). The other great mystical experience for Jesus was at the time of the transfiguration when he was received unconditionally into the company of the prophets, Moses and Elijah. Once again it is an experience of being loved, without reservations or restrictions, evoking in him a response in love which took the shape of obedience. As the baptismal experience resulted in the call to ministry, so the transfiguration experience prepared him for obedience unto the death, the crucifixion.

Such mystical experiences have the effect of raising consciousness, of heightening awareness. One is initiated into a state of consciousness known as contemplation. God is encountered internally as the God within or in the immediacy of actual physical presence, with the most intimate proximity. It is a matter of immanence, here and now, "nearer than breathing, nearer than hands and feet". It is indeed a baptism by fire. To borrow Robert Frost's words, "Once to have known it, nothing else will do. All our days are passed awaiting its return." The rest of life is henceforth inescapably judged by this flash of illumination which puts everything in proper perspective, this plumb line requiring that all else be trued up to it.

The first and foremost Christian spiritual guide is Jesus

of Nazareth. All who have since aspired to be his disciples in spiritual guidance have come to this vocation nurtured through spiritual guidance from others and initiated through the experience of being loved, singled out and commissioned to love others with the selfsame love with which they have been loved. To be called to spiritual guidance, then, is to accept the responsibility and privilege of cultivating one's own mystical faculty, of honoring the privilege and necessity to become a contemplative, quickened by love and the guidance of another.

Though the Church was later to lay the emphasis upon preparing for a life beyond death, it is clear that Jesus was primarily concerned to introduce those he counseled, his followers, to a present state of consciousness that he described as living in the Kingdom of God. He entertained the same eschatological expectations as his contemporaries of a cataclysmic event in response to a divine fiat, precipitating the end of the present age and initiating the millennial reign of God on earth. But his own mystical experience had introduced him to an even more exciting present reality: the immediate, here-and-now experience of the Kingdom of God on earth, within individual persons, in their midst, among and between them. One could not only anticipate "everlasting" life hereafter, as the reward of obedience; one could actually experience "eternal life" here and now, what could only be called "glory". This involved a sustained awareness of the Presence, a capacity for relatedness to others, and a perception of beauty, truth, and goodness heretofore unknown and therefore unrealized.

Here we encounter Jesus the Evolver (in paleontological terms), the "sport", the Second Adam, the Son of Man, the new being. Our new evolutionary perspective (which we will consider in Chapter 3) compels us to see Jesus' intoxicated preoccupation with the present experience of the Kingdom of God on earth as a breakthrough of raised consciousness. Jesus himself would not have understood this, of course, in this frame of reference. He knew nothing of God's continuing creation on this earth through evolution. But he did experience, *satori*-fashion, an awareness of living in a milieu to which others were oblivious.

He was aware of a vastly enhanced quality of life, an interior state that also transformed relationships to others. He was clear that God had commissioned him as a prophet to proclaim and to interpret his discovery to any and all who had the capacity to understand and to respond. Hence the exuberant compulsion to create one metaphor, one parable, after another to illustrate one or another aspect of this fantastic discovery of a way to enter this new stage of being. He discerned and interpreted the laws that seemed to be operative in this "divine milieu". He was quite conscious of a certain exhilaration and exaltation. Even when it became clear that for him obedience to the laws of the present kingdom would mean probable execution, the rewards of faithfulness were so real that he persisted in this practice of the Presence. "Who for the joy that was set before him endured the cross" (Heb. 12:2).

There is no question that he saw his primary mission as trying to raise the consciousness of others to the point where they could respond to this reality, this quality of living. We can see that his own spiritual guidance of others took the form of quickening this as yet undeveloped faculty in them which we can identify as the mystical or contemplative potential. So, from the outset within the Christian phylum, spiritual guidance or direction has been inseparably associated with the mystical element in the heritage.

There have been other emphases in the Church, of course, including orthodoxy of belief and conformity of its articulation to revelation in Scripture and to the teachings of the early church fathers, hierarchical or Biblical authority, and liturgical practices. These emphases can be pursued with surprising indifference toward and even abhorrence of mystical phenomena and the insights of the mystics. They may serve to indoctrinate and to provide ways of joining and participating in the building and maintenance of the institutional church, but they miss, somehow, the essence, the reality, the consciousness of the divine milieu of which we have spoken. Spiritual guidance, on the other hand, has no meaning apart from the mystical experience of being loved by God. From this interior awakening springs the love of souls and the gift to become a curé of souls. After his experience of being loved by God Jesus had but one commandment to issue: "This is my commandment: love one another as I have loved you" (John 15:12).

The ministry of spiritual guidance has thus from its beginning, in the Christian context, concerned itself with awakening the mystical consciousness, with imparting a readiness to respond to the mystical experience of being loved by God, and with motivating another to a commitment to faithfulness and obedience that makes possible living here and now the life eternal. Paul lists this talent for guidance among the gifts of the Spirit: "those who have gifts of healing, or ability to help others or power to guide them" (I Cor. 12:28). But it was to be many centuries before a distinctive ministry of spiritual guidance was to evolve and be recognized within the Church.

GUIDANCE AND THE INWARD JOURNEY

One can trace the more proximate beginnings of the formal practice of spiritual guidance in the emergence of the phenomenon of the desert fathers in the fourth century. In response to the experience of being loved by God and in some sense called apart by this distinction, these individuals took to the solitude of the desert. They were indeed, like their Master before them, "led by the Spirit into the wilderness to be tempted" (Matt. 4:1). Once led, however, they remained to practice the eremitic life and to make themselves available to any who pursued them into the desert in quest of the spiritual guidance it was rumored they could offer. So began the linkage between the monastic life and spiritual direction with the vocation of the "religious" men and women committed to celibacy, poverty, and obedience as a way of life. Not that spiritual direction is not especially needed if one aspires to this vocation. But this association was unfortunate, first in preempting the word "religious" for members of monastic orders and second in the implication that the laity, not being among the "religious", had no need of spiritual direction. What we can now see is that for a Christian the important vocation is to be a contemplative, involving cultivation of the mystical faculty, whether he or she be lay or professional with reference to the institutional church. It is a matter of initiation through the experience of being loved by God, perhaps through another human being, as the author of the Fourth Gospel experienced the love of God through Jesus' love for him. This is followed by a response in love taking the form of a passionate desire to be obedient to the will of the One who first loved us. This sequence in turn makes evident one's own need for help, while pursuing this path of obedience, in becoming a contemplative, whatever one's place or station in the common life. As we have seen, even the Catholic Church has not felt the responsibility, traditionally, to afford the laity ready access to this kind of spiritual direction. Most Protestant churches have not, until recently, felt the need to provide such a ministry even to the clergy and professional church workers, much less the laity. Clergy are ordained to a ministry of "Word and Sacrament", not to one of spiritual guidance. This may be just as well, since only a small percentage of the clergy are endowed with this gift of guidance, whereas some unordained laypersons are richly blessed with it.

THE BEGINNINGS OF THE FORMAL PRACTICE

From the time of the desert fathers on, there is a clearly delineated vocation of spiritual direction. A tradition is gradually established, and a succession of curés of souls begins to form. Augustine initiated in his *Confessions* a kind of reflection upon the inward journey that was a forerunner of the practice of journal-keeping, a logging of the milestones on one's own spiritual pilgrimage. Further, he began a study of the elements of progression in the pursuit of the mystic or contemplative way that was to be reexamined and confirmed by the great succession of mystics that followed, whose ministry was primarily spiritual guidance. Throughout the long historical succession of mystics there has been consensus about the developmental stages in the journey: purgation, illumination, unitive life.

For anyone intent upon pursuing the inward journey to the self and to the Self, it became immediately clear that there were certain universal besetting impediments to progress. These included moral duplicity or turpitude, anger and resultant violence, inordinate desires and affections, jealousy and covetousness, ennui and lethargy, and so on. One could not even effectively embark on the life of the spirit as long as these roadblocks stood in the way. One needed a director or guide to help identify the existence of these barriers and to assist in their exorcism through prayer, fasting, and penance.

Once some initial purging had taken place, one could undertake the disciplines of illumination which included reflection on Scripture and devotional classics, meditative and contemplative prayer, more profound participation in the sacraments, and active identification with the body of Christ, the church militant, especially the monastic order to which one belonged. The ultimate goal was the unitive life, but one was not to expect ever fully to attain this state. It was a matter of proximation. The need for further purging and illumination never really ceased. Indeed, as Kierkegaard well knew, the only vocation in which one might continue to grow in stature as long as one's faculties held was that of the penitent. But even for the penitent, there was always the need for further purging. And the process of illumination was lifelong.

The object of this arduous journey was to become a mystic, a contemplative, indeed a saint. The indisputable evidence was palpable attainment of the unitive life, whatever further qualifications (i.e., having performed at least two miracles) formal canonization might require. This attainment was thought of not as a means of winning recognition or prestige in this life, but of assuring entrance into heaven beyond death. There was also, of course, the supplemental value of an exemplary life as an influence for good upon others. But the motivation for gathering many into one fold here sprang primarily from the desire to present as many of the faithful as could be won in this manner at the Parousia, the second coming.

The journey was well marked and mapped, as indicated, in its general outline. But for every traveler the starting point was different and the combinations and permutations of hazards and assistances en route inevitably varied enormously. Those consciously on this journey knew themselves to be "pilgrims". Bunyan was later to isolate, identify, and to personify a great many of the trials and tribulations as well as the aids and supports one was almost certain to encounter at one time or another. His book was written for Protestants, but Catholics on the same journey could recognize the terrain. Perhaps this is why for a long time *Pilgrim's Progress* was the best seller in English, second only to the Bible itself.

What was not always clear was that this journey led not only to the true self within but that this true self within was also inescapably linked to the Self, God within. The journey was one journey. It is one thing to "fight the good fight" against "the world, the flesh, and the devil" in the sense of an external conflict, and to reach the destination of a committed life. This is the extravert's battle. The objective of the greatest of the spiritual guides, however, is quite another thing: to help the person unite with the God within at the heart of the citadel of the self where God and the person are one. This is the way of the mystic, the royal road of the contemplative.

UNION WITH THE GOD WITHIN

This is the joyous message of Meister Eckhart in the fourteenth century. Happily he preached it to the peasantry as well as to the "religious" in monasteries and convents, indeed to all who would give him a hearing. Again, it was with the same excitement that had characterized Jesus' discovery of what it is like to live presently in this divine milieu. One must still do battle with the enemies of the Spirit within and without. But if one were but to open his or her inward eye he or she would perceive that heaven has already been attained at the depth of one's being. One had only to become what one already was by creation and promise.

This is the central mystical truth, the heart of the matter, the burden of Jesus' prophecy. The grace of this gift of being is itself incontrovertible. It constitutes the consensus of all mystical consciousness. It is the "perennial philosophy" of the mystical strand of all the living religions. The great lover is already in residence at the center of the psyche. Whenever consciousness is sufficiently raised to apprehend this presence, the unconditional and unrestricted love is experienced inwardly. The response to this love is the experience of at-one-ment. For the moment, the stream of consciousness, what the Easterners call the "maya" of incessant change and flow, is halted. Eternity impinges upon time. There is a kind of stasis, a mystical awareness of elemental harmony running through all things. Augustine's "we are restless until we find our rest in Thee" and Julian of Norwich's "all shall be well, and all shall be well, and all manner of thing shall be well" are varied responses to one basic experience — the experience of conscious breakthrough to one divine milieu, that inner space "whose center is everywhere and whose circumference is nowhere".

But the intensity of the light is blinding. Even the inner eye cannot long endure it, as Robert Frost acknowledges in the concluding words of a poem, "Heaven gives its glimpses only to those not in position to look too close." Excess of light seems inevitably to be followed by darkness. Hence the universal experience of the dark night. John of the Cross discerns two different dark nights encountered at two different stages of the inward journey we are attempting to describe. The first, the dark night of the senses, follows victory in purging some of the more gross sins of the flesh. The dark night of the spirit, experienced later, comes unbidden as a kind of compensatory experience to one's progress in subduing some of the subtler temptations of the spirit. Both dark nights are to be endured with patience, with consolation drawn from the fact that they reflect progress on the inward journey, on the inherent principle, often enunciated, "no cross, no crown".

The radical contradiction between the mystical theology of which we speak and the prevailing historical theology of the institutional church, both Protestant and Catholic, will become apparent. Dogmatic theology has held that human nature is corrupt at the core ever since the historic "fall" in the Garden of Eden. The ultimate blame for this fallen state may be laid at the feet of Lucifer, the fallen angel, the devil. Man is in bondage to this devil until he accepts release at the hands of the Savior, Jesus of Nazareth. The death on the cross is the ransom paid the devil for the release of humankind. To change the metaphor to one of Old Testament origin, Jesus on the cross was the sacrificial lamb offered to appease an angry God. The Middle Ages gave birth to another and comparable metaphor, that of a cosmic courtroom in which humankind is in the docket, guilty of the unforgivable sin. No punishment can fit the heinous crime of incorrigible evil within. The only thing which can serve as an appropriate propitiation for man's and women's incurable state is the crucifixion of an innocent victim, Jesus of Nazareth. In all three metaphors the implication is that salvation comes by Jesus' death on the cross, the supreme propitiation for the sin of humankind, the efficacy of which is to be appropriated by a leap of faith in the believer.

For mystical theology in its classical form, on the other hand, the real condition of humankind is quite otherwise. The emphasis and perspective is not on salvation but on incarnation. Man does not simply have the potential of being saved externally. He is not simply made in the divine image and stamped out with a certain potential, awaiting a state of conversion that will afford him a redeemed status and hence admit him to the Kingdom hereafter. Rather, man and woman have been created one with God, and are a divine emanation. There is not only that in every man and woman which can, under certain circumstances, become God-like. There is actually "that of God in every man and woman", as the Friends say. The God who, as the Old Testament persists in claiming, chose to dwell in thick darkness, characteristically has chosen to dwell in the thick darkness of the unconscious in the human psyche. Meister Eckhart uses the happy image of a bubbling spring at the depths of one's own being which, though it may be overlaid and obscured by various kinds of debris, keeps indefatigably welling up from within. Nothing, not even a theoretically unforgivable sin, can staunch it. Carl Jung inscribed in stone over the entrance to his home in Kusnacht, "Called or not called, I [God] am there." That's the real condition, the most important thing that can be said of the human being, according to mystical theology.

This does not mean that one may not at the same time "make his bed in hell", as the Psalmist knew to his chagrin. But as he also discovered to his immense surprise and consolation, "If I make my bed in hell, behold Thou art there." So, salvation for one whose consciousness has been raised to the mystical level, even if only on one or two occasions, is a matter of response in love to the experience of being loved, an internal resolution to embark on this inward journey that leads to this real self within and to the Self, God within. Jesus' death on the cross has simply the meaning Jesus himself ascribed to it according to the Fourth Gospel: "Greater love hath no man than this, that a man lay down his life for his friends" (John 15:13). His love was in response to his experience of being loved by God, directed now towards the disciples as well as to God. Having known the love of God, he simply loved his own until the end.

The Church has always intuitively reacted to this doctrine of mystical theology as threatening to her own authority, not only because it was not in accord with her official statements and the teachings of her recognized theologians, but also because for the mystics the ultimate authority springs from their own mystical experiences rather *an affirming statement!*

than the Church, Scripture, the patristic fathers, or ecumenical councils. Yet, for one to whom this mystical theology speaks the eternal Word because of personal, confirming intimations or experiences, the only authentic apostolic succession is that of the mystics, the genuine contemplatives. It is this succession to which we refer when we speak of the tradition of Christian spiritual direction. The central teachings of mystical theology still stand, even in our new day. They are to be perceived in a new context within the evolving universe, but this perception further confirms their basic soundness. God dwells at the heart of every human being. Mystical consciousness reveals the paradox that this God who is totally transcendent and totally "other" is at the same moment immanent, the Self of my self.

To be saved I must simply be what I already am. This will involve an arduous inward journey, the acceptance of solitude, the pursuit of spiritual disciplines, the deliberate cultivation of the universal mystical faculty — in short, becoming a contemplative. But if I have the resolution and the stamina to embark on this journey, I shall claim the comfort of being rooted and grounded in a great heritage. I shall plant my footsteps deliberately on a well-trodden way and feel myself supported and comforted by a great company in unbroken continuity, a cloud of witnesses. Little by little I shall learn what Jesus meant about the Kingdom of God being a present reality and stake out my own little claim in this divine milieu, striving daily to lift my consciousness to become ever more aware of the way things really are.

In the next chapter we will be attentive to certain modifications and revisions of aspects of the heritage which the fresh revelation emerging from the accumulating insights of depth psychology, specifically that of Carl Jung, requires of us. We know more about some aspects of the human psyche now. It is our responsibility to inform and reform the heritage in accordance with this fresh revelation while we consciously stand firmly in unbroken continuity with that heritage.

In the third chapter we shall have the task of

assimilating this newly wrought union of the heritage and the insights of Jungian psychology within the context of "the new story", the new myth of continuing creation as it has been articulated for us in the prophetic vision of Teilhard de Chardin, a breakthrough of revelation about the cosmos as still in process of being born.

CHAPTER 2

THE RELEVANCE OF JUNG'S PSYCHOLOGY

The unbroken continuity of Christian spiritual direction has been concerned with the care and nurture of the psyche on its journey through this "troublous" life to its destination in eternity. As we shall point out in the next chapter, the nature of the journey, and even, in a sense, its destination must now be seen in an altogether different light in view of the new evolutionary perspective. But meantime we want to focus on the way in which our understanding of the human psyche has been radically and irrevocably changed by the accumulative insights of depth psychology, especially those of Carl Jung. "Standing on the shoulders of Freud", as he knew himself to be, he was nevertheless enabled thereby to see further into reality and to perceive convergences of which Freud, whose knowledge of history and philosophy was more limited, was unaware.

ARCHETYPES AND THE COLLECTIVE UNCONSCIOUS

Jung, of course, accepted the Darwinian findings in the *Origin of Species*. Persuaded by Freud of the enormous and central importance of the unconscious as the reservoir of repression and the focus for study of the pathology of the psyche, he went far beyond his early mentor in probing the potential recall on an evolutionary scale through the existence of what he called "the collective unconscious". Jung saw this as reaching down through successive expanding strata of the personal unconscious, the national or racial unconscious, even the psyche's inarticulate beginnings in humanity's animal forebears. This collective unconscious is the conduit through which the archetypes play their important role in keeping the developing, conscious psyche "on course". It is as if the archetypes represent the accumulated wisdom in certain areas of development, the personified standards or norms that preserve the experience of the past in the evolution of the psyche, finding its way to where it is now, still in transit to an ultimate destination we know not of.

The archetyes, the wise old man, the wise old woman, the child, the devil, the Christ, the anima, the animus, these idealizations or caricatures, as the case may be, appear in dreams and fantasies to convey important messages. They can tell us when we are off course or in need of discerning the next step on our journey. Their messages, properly understood, can represent the still small voice of God within. But it can be disastrous fully to identify with any one of them. Rather, they serve to move us back into place when we wander. They are like guard rails on a highway, keeping us from going over the cliff. Moreover, they remind us where we've been in the past and direct us in our forward journey.

From the religious point of view this is a profound mystery. It is as if the mysterious God, who is both transcendent to and immanent within creation, were working his or her way through a kind of infinite possibility into specific incarnations through the guidance provided by God's own Word in the shape of archetypes. We shall see, later on, that a paradox is involved. While archetypes reflect a certain continuity in terms of standardization and normalization, there is also a factor of unpredictability and spontaneity that is always working toward differentiation and that bears fruit in new species. One can see this as a kind of "divine dalliance" or playfulness. This is yet another expression in the divine countenance that is forever changing. Exclaimed Teilhard, "God has a new face: the evolutive God of cosmogenesis."

Jung saw that these two factors of continuity and spontaneity were both involved with reference to the journey of the individual psyche. The archetypes, we have said, are rooted in the collective unconscious of the species and these roots extend down even into the subsoil of our animal forebears and beyond. We lose their trail in the heart of matter when we attempt to follow them backward in time. They emerge and play upon elements in the personal or what Jung sometimes called the "objective" unconscious of the individual, that combination of potential gifts and weaknesses that constitute one's uniqueness. It is perhaps in this mysterious interplay, fleeting glimpses of which are exposed in dreams and fantasies, that the drive toward the miracle of differentiation has its opportunity.

No doubt our very genes· have programmed certain limitations as well as potentialities in our development. They undoubtedly have had a determining voice in the shaping of our psychological type which, in the Jungian sense, means whether we are to be introverts or extraverts, whether our dominant function is to be thinking, feeling, intuiting, or sensing. But there remains a vast area of unpredictability, a thick darkness from which unexpected refracted light may emerge. Something in the individual human being wants us to be both recognizably human and at the same time different (differentiated) from all other human beings that have ever lived. Could this be God, seeking ever new forms of existence for himself/herself?

THE NEW TASK OF RELIGION

However this may be, religion has been assigned an enormous new task by the psychology of C. G. Jung. The Latin derivation of the very word (*religo-religare*) connotes "binding into one sheaf or bundle". Of all our instincts, it is the most profound and the most comprehensive. As we shall see in the next chapter, it is the built-in function that serves the very process of evolution itself. Evolution makes one basic demand of all its creatures: assimilate or perish. In the contemporary vernacular it might be put this way: "Get it all together or fail to reach your potential." Until the advent of depth psychology, the Christian heritage understood that religion required one to order and harmonize one's relationships, to interrelate body and mind and spirit as one whole, to reach for simplicity of life amid the encircling complexity and threatening dissociation. But no one ever dreamed that a fresh revelation of the importance of the unconscious would, in the name of religion, demand that we make conscious its contents and then integrate that with the contents of consciousness. What an expansion of religious responsibility! The prospect is a little daunting, to say the least. Yet, just as the mountain that is "there" gives no rest until it is climbed, so the unconscious that has been discovered to be "there" will afford no peace until it has been plumbed and integrated.

Before we move on to other elements in Jung's psychology we must recognize further that in an evolving universe these mysterious inherent forces known as archetypes, often personified in dreams and fantasies, not only preserve a continuity with the past as evolution moves forward, but also prompt endless experimentations producing new differentiations. In some unknown way, they have something to do with carrying the seed of future species of which we cannot presently even dream. But if we cannot see the distant scene, we can at least see the lineaments of the next development in the human species, the emerging "homo spiritus" of whom Jesus of Nazareth is the "sport", the first-born among many brethren, the Second Adam, the

Son of Man. "You won't know who I am unless the Father reveals it to you" (John 6:65), that is, "the Holy Spirit who dwells within you". "Unless the Christ archetype in you confirms the Christ incarnation in me you won't recognize me as the Way, the Truth, and the Life." "Unless what's crying out to be given life in you responds with a resounding yea to what has been given life in me, you won't passionately cry out like Pilgrim, 'Life, Life', and bend your energies in hot pursuit." As Angelus Silesius expressed it in the seventeenth century,

> Though Christ a thousand times
> In Bethlehem be born
> If he's not born in thee
> Thy soul is still forlorn.[1]

Until the arrival of depth psychology we had been unaware of the existence of a vast area of life in the psyche: the unconscious. We recollect the great counsel of a passage in the Old Testament: "I have set before you this day life and death. Therefore choose life" (Dt. 30:19). Now we are confronted with the ancient challenge in a new form: "I have set before you this day the unconscious and raised consciousness. Therefore choose raised consciousness." Herein, as we shall presently see, not only lies the way of individuation, but also the "royal way of the holy cross". More of this later.

Such fresh revelation calls for a radical revision of some of the presuppositions on which spiritual guidance has been based. Spiritual guidance practiced within the context of an evolving universe and subject to the operation of evolution's laws appears quite different from its practice within a static framework.

One difference is that in an evolving universe there can be no discontinuity between this world and the next, life this side of death, and life beyond. As life moves on, "one never steps into the same river twice". It becomes more difficult, in an evolutionary continuum, to conceive of life hereafter as ceaselessly chanting in a heavenly chorus or rendering endless variations on a single theme with a harp that never needs tuning (if we are fortunate enough to be assigned to a place of eternal bliss), or as being buried in unending flames or the deep freeze of individual potholes (to recall Dore's visualizations of Dante's *Inferno*).

It is inconceivable that a part of the universe evolves and another part does not. The "ultimate concern" or "anxiety" would seem of necessity to be different in our day. It is no longer whether hereafter I should be assigned permanently to heaven or hell. It is whether I retain my individuality, proving viable by way of hard-won integration for further evolved consciousness, or devolve into nothingness, dissolution, oblivion, returning to the original chaos from which across aeons of time I sprang. This shift in concern alters everything, because in a new sense when I commit wrong I not only disobey God, but also thwart the creative process which is even now at work in my interior parts. Denying God is not only rebellion against a transcendent Being but a flagrant rejection of something, Someone, deep within me who is my *raison d'être*.

Another striking difference between the assumptions of the heritage and the new perception of the human psyche concerns the ancient myth of the Fall and the source of continuing temptation. According to the tradition, one can pinpoint in time the source of man's proclivity for evil. It happened when the first man and woman were living happily in a Garden of Eden. A serpent tempted Eve to eat the apple, the fruit of the tree of the knowledge of good and evil. She in turn beguiled Adam with this Faustian temptation, and he, too, yielded. This is the source of original sin, it is claimed, the reason for man's cleft will, inherited by all men and women from that time forward. Behind this myth lies the other myth that the devil, personified by the snake, was a fallen angel. He is to be recognized as a ravening wolf, "going about seeking whom he may devour". The question is not even raised as to why there could be any defection, in the first place, of a creature who owed its very existence to the loving and all-powerful God. At any rate, God now has an enemy, a powerful enemy, not strong enough to threaten God's existence, but strong enough to lure away from God many of his creatures, even to destruction.

From the point of view of the Jungian myth of the

psyche, the ancient myths represent understandable projections from the unconscious of what is in reality an interior condition of the human psyche. The proximate source of evil is man himself. But from an evolutionary perspective this is not something that just began in a specific locale, the Garden of Eden, at a given time, with a fatal blunder that could afflict all men and women thereafter. The principle of unbroken continuity in evolution carries us back in our quest for the source to the beginning of time. There is no stopping point. The divine economy itself allows for the possibility of evil.

It is the mystic, the philosophic monist, in Jung and Teilhard that causes them to lay ultimate responsibility for the presence of evil in the universe at the feet of the Creator. Teilhard suggests that it is the price God had to pay for the very process of continuing creation through evolution. Below the level of sentience, evil, he holds, is statistical failure to realize new forms of union; above the level of sentience, evil is the failure to realize union through forgiveness, reconciliation, communion and community by reason of the seven deadly sins. Jung, at certain points in his writing, wants to convert the Trinity into a quaternity (mandala) in which evil is considered part of the Godhead, the shadow side of God, if you will. This proposal, of course, gives rise to theological problems with which we will come to terms later.

COPING WITH EVIL IN AUTONOMOUS COMPLEXES

For the present, though neither evolution nor depth psychology can provide any answers to the ultimate problem of evil — why it should be present at all in the creation of an all-powerful and all-loving God — we are forced by these new revelations to see how indigenous evil is within the whole process of evolution. It is not something that can be righted once and for all by the death of an innocent victim on a cross. One has to acknowledge the omnipresence of the demonic in the psyche, identify one's own shadow manifestations, discern and do battle with the enemy within, the evil urge that would work our undoing. We can say that in Teilhardian terms evil is what thwarts the forward movement in evolution toward higher consciousness and that in Jungian terms evil is that which impedes or precludes growth toward wholeness in the human psyche.

We can learn from depth psychology that self-flagellation, the wearing of a hairshirt, and severe penances can be counterproductive in the quest of wholeness of life. When one has apparently banished one demon, seven more deadly ones may suddenly appear. On the other hand it is an over-simplification to hold, as some psychologists do, that wholeness is simply a matter of befriending one's demons and performing some kind of moral jujitsu. It is more than a matter of inviting the demons in for a figurative "cup of tea" in order to talk things over and negotiate a truce. I must own my evil proclivities as part of me and by some kind of recognition seek to divert their destructive energies to some more creative purpose. It may prove fatal either to deny their existence or to set out, like St. George, to slay the dragon altogether. A spiritual guide, informed by depth psychology, will want to help his or her counselee to identify the demons within as well as without, and to learn how to keep them at bay, if not transform them.

When a woman asked Abraham Lincoln why he did not destroy his enemies instead of making them his friends, Lincoln responded, "What, madam, do I not destroy my enemies when I make them my friends?" As long as we do not take this counsel too literally, or as applying universally to all demons, it has profound relevance to the spiritual guidance of which we are speaking. Bear in mind, however, that there are some demons which, unless vanquished or disarmed, have the power to destroy. Our concern here is to point out that the ancient technique of exorcism, though apparently still efficacious in the charismatic movement, raises contemporary doubts concerning the permanence of the miracles it claims and its efficacy as a mode of coping with evil. We are increasingly aware that a frontal attack by the will may appear to produce immediate results and yet simultaneously cause undesirable side effects. It is one thing if the source of evil is an external being, the devil, who seeks to overpower us. It is quite another if the source is to be found in shadow manifestations that are inherently part of the psyche itself. In one case a direct encounter would seem indicated. In the other an attempt to destroy the enemies by befriending them, within limits, seems a viable approach.

One of Jung's insights is that a particularly dangerous enemy can take the form of what he called an "autonomous complex", "autonomous" because it creates an independent orbit of its own within the psyche, "complex" because it characteristically tends to pull into its orbit other parts of the psyche. In this way it becomes a pretender to the throne of identity, threatening the wholeness and integrity of the individual. This complex may form around any of a number of human emotions such as anger, unrelinquished hostility, jealousy, anxiety, overweening ambition, grief, greed, or inordinate attachment. If it has sufficient gravitational pull, it throws everything else out of balance. One knows one is dealing with an autonomous complex when one feels beside oneself, possessed, torn to pieces, and well-laid plans are arbitrarily changed to meet, in some sinister way, the demands of this complex. Depth psychology attempts to track down to its lair the source of such dis-ease in the psyche and to identify its root cause. This is a critical step in eliminating the symptoms, which can be quite devastating and which all too often are rationalized away as springing from something else because the psyche does not want to look at the real source.

PERSONA AND SHADOW

We have been alluding to the shadow and to shadow manifestations as constituting demonic forces within the psyche. It was Carl Jung's conviction that in direct proportion to the intensity with which one consciously or unconsciously accepted a persona — (an image of how one desires to be perceived by others) — there would be a compensating opposite tendency in the unconscious, accompanied by potentially dangerous energy in the psyche. This same principle of compensation, a kind of built-in symmetry in the internal structure of the psyche, applies especially in the area of one's best gifts. The worst temptations and shadow manifestations are always related to one's best gifts.

Paul Tournier in *The Violence Within* identifies and describes an impulse to exercise power on the part of all those in the helping professions. This urge, if unrecognized and therefore unresisted, leads to the unconscious practice of violence on the psyches of others. A charismatic gift can easily be subverted into an unconscious exercise of violence in the inebriation of power. This dynamic has been depicted dramatically in Elmer Gantry and Mar-Jo and played out in real life by Jim Jones of Guyana and other contemporary counterparts whose persona is charismatic religious leader or guru. Their shadow, once called into play, can work havoc in the lives of others.

We recall Jesus' own temptations in the wilderness. Was not this peculiar dynamic in the psyche responsible for them? They all had to do with the abuse of power, accompanying the role of messiah, winning response and acclaim by false means: leaping unharmed from the pinnacle of the temple, turning stones into bread, compromising with principle. The common projection points a finger at an external devil, but the culprit can be internalized and seen clearly to reside within. Jesus, if fully human, must have had a shadow. Indeed, from the depth-psychological point of view, the most horrendous "anti-Christ" is not some benighted historical figure we might nominate, but the shadow in the psyche of Jesus of Nazareth.

So well recognized and dependable is this dangerous dynamic that one may be sure of its secret operation in the psyche and be well advised deliberately to look for one's own shadow manifestations, related to one's own best gifts, lest they gang up and overtake one, unaware, in a most disastrous way. Those with the heaviest personas will be found inevitably to harbor within, quite unconsciously, the most dangerous shadows. Let the pastor and spiritual guide beware! There is no heavier persona than the "man or woman of God" or the "friend of God". The one designation more dangerous still is that of "saint". Happily, canonization is not accorded save posthumously, a stroke of genius on the part of a Church that has not always been distinguished for its wisdom. Leon Bloy was speaking of the unattained aspiration only when he wrote, "There is only one sorrow: not to be a saint." While we know intuitively whereof he spoke and the safeguard of humility his words reflect, we also recognize that to court realization of this awesome status in the shape of a persona is psychologically the most dangerous form of identification with an archetype, the ultimate inflation.

Since the acknowledged goal of the pursuit of sanctity in Christian history was actually sainthood, many of those throughout the Christian heritage who embarked on this hazardous journey had no conception of the dangers they were running. The very magnitude of their aspirations, however, often revealed to them that they were, in their own sight, the most miserable of sinners. Apart from some such instinctive sense of the precariousness of their course and their accompanying precautions, would-be saints were without exception riding for a fall. In any case, informed by this demonstrable insight emerging from depth psychology, we are at least armed against some of the pitfalls that afflicted some of our forerunners in the faith. A contemporary spiritual guide can impart to the counselee an occasional pertinent warning and encourage the cultivation of a practiced wariness.

THE ANIMA AND ANIMUS

Jung had a very strong conviction that wholeness was the only viable holiness of life. Pursuing holiness must take into account the opposites that inevitably exist in the psyche and the necessity to strive for a conjunction of those opposites rather than one-sided emphases that produce an insecure balance. One of his most fruitful insights was that every man has within his psyche a feminine component which he designated the "anima", and likewise every woman a masculine component he named the "animus". These can be seen as compensatory factors in the symmetry of the psyche. Another way of putting this aspect of the dynamism within the psyche is to say that every man carries within him his own Eve and every woman her Adam.

There is much contemporary protest against this particular tenet of Jung's psychology. It is maintained by some that there are no such realities as distinguishable masculine or feminine psychic components, only characteristics which the imposition of cultural customs and mores have falsely designated as masculine or feminine. While recognizing the enormous influence of cultural practice and association in our perception of what is masculine and feminine, and the wide range of variation between individuals as well as cultures from an anthropological view, I must confess that Jung's argument is basically persuasive to me. In a delicate mechanism like the human body-mind-spirit entity it seems highly unlikely that the important biological differences and functions in men and women would not have their psychological counterparts.

So I hold with Jung that there are such realities as psychological characteristics that are prevailingly masculine or feminine. At the same time in a psyche whose very survival depends on achieving and maintaining a viable wholeness, integration, balance, it is essential to recognize the existence of the contra-sexual component within the psyche and deliberately to cultivate it, to raise it into consciousness. Irene Claremont de Castillejo defined the masculine component as "focused consciousness", or the ability to discriminate, differentiate, categorize. The feminine component she described as "diffuse awareness", an awareness of the unity and inter-relatedness of all life. Jung suggested in *Two Essays on Analytical Psychology* that the individual undertake from time to time, as an exercise in active imagination, an actual dialogue, the man with his anima, the woman with her animus, particularly in their identifiable negative manifestations, the shadow side.

Of course these do not exist as detached beings in the psyche. Just as Jung pleads with the Church in *The Undiscovered Self* that she understand her dogmas "metaphorically, just for once", so he would be the first to insist that one is to understand all the elements of his psychology as integral parts of a myth of the psyche, to be taken only metaphorically. The important thing is to be aware of the dynamics involved and to preserve a sense of one's center, the self, in creative dialogue with the parts, to the end of realizing wholeness. From the point of view of the heritage of Christian spiritual guidance, the new element that has been introduced is a higher consciousness of the complexity within the psyche, its built-in opposites, persona and shadow, anima and animus, and the need to strive for a conjunction of opposites.

THE QUEST OF THE HOLY GRAIL: INDIVIDUATION

The central and basic dynamic within the psyche which is the instinctive striving of the self toward wholeness Jung names the process of individuation. He was persuaded, as we have seen, that wholeness was the only viable holiness of life; all other quixotic attempts to take this heaven by storm are doomed to self-deception and ultimate failure. As an indication of the importance he attached to this inward journey and the numinous light in which he saw it, he chose the most romantic metaphor from Christian religious literature to symbolize it: the quest of the Holy Grail. He meant to suggest that no enterprise could be fraught with more high adventure nor be more profoundly religious. It is the soul's supreme responsibility; no one else can undertake it on behalf of another. "Unless I do it, it won't get done."

In *The Undiscovered Self* Jung suggests there is only one condition in which it would be the better part of valor to forego this inward journey. This condition is when the given individual, drawn to the adventure, has not sufficient self-acceptance and self-love to withstand the dangers; that is to say, when one has not sufficiently experienced the love of God as an unconditional and unrestricted love so that one can entrust oneself with a measure of confidence to endure the very considerable risks involved. One thinks of Lady Macbeth's discovery, "Hell is murky, m'Lord." Though one seeks a heaven within, hell in the shape of lurking demons that can destroy, the threat of dissociation, meaninglessness, and nothingness must also be traversed. Will one have the stamina to encounter, without headlong flight or overpowering temptations to self-destruction (Freud's death wish), these dark figures who are part of one's own psyche?

When Jung decided to take the plunge, baptizing himself by immersion in the unconscious (a profoundly religious act, perhaps a new sacrament), he was fully aware of the enormous risk he was taking: that he might not return unscathed and sane. He had been the recipient of what would be understood as warning dreams and fantasies. But his resolve held fast. First, as long as the unconscious was there, he was mystically drawn to plumb its depths, and second, he was passionately convinced that "only the wounded physician heals." If he would serve his patients, he must know something more than vicarious imagination afforded of that dark land from whence suffering and neuroses emerge. So, he said to himself, in fear and trembling, "Well, Jung old boy, here you go," and plunged in, knowing full well that this was a voyage from whose bourne some travelers had not returned.

JUNG'S CALL TO BE A CURÉ OF SOULS

I have said that before one even considers an interior call to become a spiritual guide, one must needs have been visited by intimations, even if not vivid and unforgettable reassurances, that one is profoundly loved by God. In his autobiography *Memories, Dreams, Reflections,* Jung shares what constitute, it seems to me, his initiatory and qualifying experiences. Three of them came very early. It was only later, in maturity, that he identified their basically positive nature as confirmation by God that he was accepted, indeed loved.

The first was a very early dream (indeed Jung was only three years of age) of an underground, phallic God, a dream which had inherent elements of terror, but whose atmosphere was one of beauty, mystery and wonder. Later he came to see it as conveying a message that the body and the unconscious also reflected the numinous and bore witness to their own divine origin.

A few years afterward he was visited by a horrendous fantasy of God smashing his church (symbolized by a cathedral) with his own defecation, a thought for which, given his background and his father's indirect teaching, he felt he must be struck by lightning. Fearing he had committed the "unforgivable sin", he entertained the neurotic notion that he could not allow himself to think this thought, although in point of fact he already had. A period of inevitable neurosis followed this repression, prompted by his guilt. Then, in despair, but actually visited by grace, he allowed himself to think the unthinkable, and there ensued a great release. No lightning struck; indeed, a miraculous calm was bestowed upon him. It was a curious kind of mystical experience. It was as if God had said, "Nothing you can do or even think can take you beyond my love and care," a curious and mild equivalent of "This is my beloved son in whom I am well pleased."

Finally, there was the mystical experience between the ages of seven and nine of sitting on a rock, not knowing where he ended and the rock began, aware of a strange interpenetration.

> And then began an imaginary game that went something like this: 'I am sitting on top of this stone and it is underneath.' But the stone also could say 'I' and think: 'I am lying here on this slope and he is sitting on top of me.' The question then arose:

'Am I the one who is sitting on the stone, or am I the stone on which *he* is sitting?' This question always perplexed me, and I would stand up, wondering who was what now.[2]

This sense of the interpenetration of all things and of somehow identifying not only with other persons also but with other things is a characteristic of mystical experience. One of its effects is thereafter to feel singularly at home and unafraid in the universe.

One other experience is important to recall in this context. When Jung was in his early twenties, he decided on medicine as a vocation but realized he would have to specialize. The decision weighed heavily on him. Then, while reading a book by Krafft-Ebing on psychiatry, he came across a passage in which the author referred to psychoses as "diseases of the personality". Jung shares with us at this point an important confession:

My heart suddenly began to pound. I had to stand up and draw a deep breath. My excitement was intense, for it had become clear to me, in a flash of illumination, that for me the only possible goal was psychiatry.[3]

Jung explicitly trusted this kind of intuition. Surely it reflects a hard-won confidence in himself, a feeling that he could trust his own daimon, the still small voice within. This confidence does not come except by way of growing certitude that one is acceptable and even lovable because one has been loved.

So Jung became one of the great curés of souls and stood in that succession, whether he would have acknowledged this or not. He felt "confirmed" in his vocation. It is not too much to say that he experienced a kind of ordination from on high for this purpose. In the words of Gerard Manley Hopkins, "For this was I born, for this I came into the world."

Depth psychology provides new criteria by which one can discern the authenticity of the gift in one's self and in others. To have experienced in some form being loved without restriction or reservation by the great Lover of souls, this is the preeminent qualification. This it is which not only beckons to the vocation but constitutes the ground on which one may take the risk of embarking on the inward journey involving in large part the quest for wholeness, the task of consciousness raising which is the way of individuation. How indeed shall one guide others on the inward journey to the self and to the Self unless one has had the courage and the stamina to undertake this journey oneself? Nor does the journey ever end. Before one may presume to guide another, one must have spent a number of years on the perilous voyage. This, of course, always has been the case throughout the history of Christian spiritual direction. But more is known now, through the discipline of depth psychology, of the unexpected shoals, the hazardous reefs and straits, the "Scylla and Charybdis", symbolic of relentless opposites to be encountered on this voyage which, if one will but persevere, will ultimately lead all the way home.

CHAPTER 3

SPIRITUAL GUIDANCE AND THE TEILHARDIAN VISION

We have already alluded to the fact that our new evolutionary perspective has radically altered our perception of what precisely is happening in the process of spiritual guidance. The classic view saw this life as a vale of soul-making, a time of preparation for a life beyond where one could anticipate rewards or punishments according to one's faithfulness to the precepts promulgated by the Church on the authority of Scripture and the Church Fathers. It was largely a spatial concept divided by the meridian of death. We are in process of shifting now to a time concept in which we see ourselves as a present incarnation within a continuing creation that reaches back in a linear sense to the beginning of time (if time can be said to have had any beginning, a philosophical question beyond the scope of our present study). Instead of life here being a sorrowful struggle against an alien world to prepare us for a friendlier place, we begin to catch a glimpse of "the good earth" and, with reference to our life upon it, many of us would resonate to Robert Frost's wistful reflection: "I don't know where it's likely to go much better."

THE IMPORTANCE OF THE NEW PERSPECTIVE

According to the form of the funeral service in the Book of Common Prayer, at the time of the committal of the body to the ground the priest says, "earth to earth, ashes to ashes, dust to dust". As the fact of evolution has been gradually assimilated, we have begun to see something of the profundity of the implications of what was heretofore a largely unexamined metaphor. As far as we know, what is happening on this planet, on the good earth, may not be approximated anywhere else in the universe, though we should have to hold that wherever in the universe conditions have approximated those at the advent of life on this earth, life would have sprung into being. The peculiar combination of ecological factors prevailing when life emerged on this planet would produce life anywhere else. It is a uni-verse with the same laws operating throughout. We live in a post-Darwinian era as surely as we live in a post-Galilean and post-Copernican era, and there's no going back. Teilhard raises the relevant question and gives definitive answer:

Is evolution a theory, a system or a hypothesis? It is much more: it is a general condition to which all theories, all hypotheses, all systems must bow and which they must satisfy henceforward if they are to be thinkable and true. Evolution is a light illuminating all facts, a curve that all lines must follow.[4]

I do not think the claim is excessive, though it is certainly comprehensive and all-encompassing. The lines of our understanding of what is happening in the conception and practice of spiritual guidance must begin to follow this curve. Teilhard goes on to say:

What makes and classifies a 'modern' man (and a whole host of our contemporaries is not yet modern in this sense) is having become capable of

> seeing in terms not of space and time alone, but also
> of duration, or — and it comes to the same thing
> — of biological space-time; and above all having
> become incapable of seeing anything otherwise,
> anything, not even himself.[5]

We should want to add, "not even spiritual guidance". To the incontrovertible continuity Darwin perceived in the succession of life on this planet, every present species being traceable backward in time to an ultimate common ancestry with all other species, Teilhard added a great new hypothesis which constitutes a new creation story or myth. Darwin was content to demonstrate that there was an integrated tree of life uniting the flora and fauna, including man, in common ancestry. From this demonstrable and well-documented picture of interrelationship which Darwin had drawn, and influenced by Henri Bergson's philosophical assimilation, Teilhard derived his perception of biological space-time or duration. But he was not content to have it begin with the first cells and end with the present. The vision of a continuing creation in which every new thing grows organically out of what had been present before demanded that questions be asked about the connection between pre-life and life. Must not the same principle of continuity prevail? Must not life emerge from structures of pre-life in the same way that more advanced life clearly springs from simpler forms? How can there conceivably be any discontinuity?

THE SHAKING OF THE FOUNDATIONS

Initially, Teilhard's faith was shaken as he began to behold a world which, in some critical respects, seemed to contradict the contours of the world which Aristotelian-Thomistic scholasticism had taught him. The world of Christian revelation was a static world of eternal verities. There existed in it an irreducible dichotomy between matter and spirit. But once the world was viewed through the lenses of biological space-time, everything changed. How reconcile the God of evolution with the Judaeo-Christian God? Consider the extravagant waste in a creation process that could tolerate one species preying upon another and some species becoming extinct, never to return. To what purpose all this meaningless waste, violence and suffering? The new perspective was a dizzying one, producing disorientation, what Teilhard called the "malady of space-time". He further articulated the ultimate doubt to which the new perception subjected us: will this process have a "suitable outcome"? Is it going anywhere, and if there seems to be a direction, what are the chances it will arrive? He diagnosed this persistent doubt as the "sickness of the dead end" and described it as our contemporary condition.

THE DISCOVERY OF "MAXIMUM COHERENCE"

Teilhard arrived at his own ultimate optimism via two routes: scientific observation and mystical experience. One thing all of Teilhard's companions in the field noticed about him was the keenness and the sharp focus of his powers of observation. He seemed to have a gift for remembering details on which he could later draw, as from an encyclopedia, in studying a specimen which he was seeking to identify at the moment. Moreover, he had an enormous capacity for concentration. And he had made an early commitment to accept truth arrived at by empirical observation, the process of scientific research.

> If, as a result of some interior revolution, I were successfully to lose my faith in Christ, my faith in a personal God, my faith in the Spirit, I think I would still believe in the World. The World (the value, the infallibility, the goodness of the World): that, in the last analysis, is the first and last thing in which I believe. It is by this faith that I live, and it is to this faith, I feel, that at the moment of death,

> mastering all doubts, I shall surrender myself. . . . I
> surrender myself to this undefined faith in a single
> and infallible World, wherever it may lead me.[6]

Committed to this loyalty as a scientist, he gave himself single-mindedly to the process of research, which he was one day to call a form of adoration. He describes for us what happened as a result. He came at length to what he discerned as the "complement and necessary corrective" to the "malady of space-time" and the "sickness of the dead end". It was, as he called it, "the perception of an evolution animating these dimensions".

> Indeed time and space become humanized as
> soon as a definite movement appears which gives
> them a physiognomy. We have only to think and
> to walk in the direction of which the lines passed
> by evolution take on their maximum coherence.[7]

When one deliberately thought and walked in this direction, the operation of an infallible law revealed itself. Teilhard named this the "law of complexity consciousness". There is a discernible direction in evolution with the accompanying promise of a "suitable outcome". Experiment and chance still play their part, but as a whole the process reveals itself as one of "*directed* chance". Evolution always moves from simpler forms to more complex ones. This is true, first, in its pre-life course: from sub-atomic particles to atoms; from atoms to molecules; from mega-molecules to cells. When life arrives, in the unbroken continuity, the factor of consciousness must be added and the process designated "complexity consciousness". As the complexity becomes even greater, reaching its present peak on this planet in man, the integration is ever more extraordinary.

Teilhard's basic insight, from which he derived his myth of cosmogenesis, is that life evolved out of what we have always called inanimate matter, but which from its inception in its most primitive form contained the seed of life. This planet has literally *grown* life, ultimately human life. We have sprung from the bowels of the earth. There has been no artificial insemination from outside, no external imposition of life upon an alien environment, the earth. We are not "strangers and pilgrims" here as the Biblical metaphor insists. We could not be more at home. It has been our *metier* from the beginning. We must now trace our ancestry backward in time not merely to the first cell moving on the face of the deep (the warmer seas that covered more of the earth's surface at the advent of life), but right back through the core of evolving matter to the birth of the earth itself. We must go back further still to the birth of the gallactic system and beyond as the linear process, read backward, recedes into the darkness of primordial space-time.

Teilhard was obliged to define the axis of this process of continuing creation within the whole panoply of time as complexity consciousness, because he perceived that consciousness was present from the beginning (if it could be said that there was any beginning) in however primitive a form. Consciousness all the way down into the heart of matter! This means spirit all the way down into the heart of matter, and no dichotomy such as even the Bible accepted. This exciting perception made Teilhard reach for one metaphor after another, one parable after another, as had Jesus with regard to the Kingdom of God on earth. "Spirit sprang from the womb of matter," he wrote, "matter is the only chalice that can hold the wine of spirit."

In addition to the scientific practice of studying the "without" of things (measuring what presented itself to the five senses), science must now take account of the "within" of things, Teilhard insisted. The "within" is the potential for higher consciousness made possible through greater complexity and leading consequently to heightened interiorization. Alpha and Omega are mysteriously one. What is to be revealed, to become incarnate, is already contained within by promise, actually realized in essence, the way the mighty oak tree is present in the acorn. God is both immanent and transcendent. The God within points to, anticipates, and does obeisance to the God ahead. This is the vision, the new creation story or myth that unfolded in the mind and heart of Teilhard as he followed his own commitment "to think and to walk in the direction in which the lines passed by evolution take on their maximum coherence".

THE CONFIRMATION OF A RECURRING MYSTICAL EXPERIENCE

We have said that Teilhard arrived at his ultimate optimism via two routes: scientific observation and mystical experience. We have seen the maximum coherence he arrived at when pursuing faithfully the lines passed by evolution. But there was also available to Teilhard another way of knowing that provided confirmation of the first. In addition to applying discursive reasoning in seeking the meaning of his scientific observations, Teilhard was visited by direct mystical experience, which for him infallibly confirmed his scientific research. He shares this recurring experience with characteristic modesty in a footnote in *The Divine Milieu*:

> Throughout my life, by means of my life, the world has little by little caught fire in my sight until, aflame all around me, it has become almost completely luminous from within. Such has been my experience in contact with the earth — the diaphany of the Divine at the heart of the universe on fire; Christ, his heart, a fire capable of penetrating everywhere and, gradually, spreading everywhere.[8]

In *Hymn to the Universe* Teilhard shares the mystical experience from which sprang his "Mass on the World", and three other wartime experiences which read as though they happened to another (they are presented as "Three Stories in the Style of Benson") but which are clearly autobiographical. All reflect the higher consciousness of a developed mystic. It was this mystical or contemplative faculty which enabled him to reconcile his scientific enquiries and his allegiance to Christian revelation as a priest. His myth of cosmogenesis and its corollary, Christogenesis, emerged as his scientific studies were irradiated by his Christian faith. In his interpretation of an evolutive creation, Teilhard has provided us with the basis of a great synthesis, many of the details of which are still to be worked out.

CRITIQUE OF TEILHARD'S CHRISTOLOGY

My own conviction is that, despite his declared intention of making revelation yield to scientific observation — ultimate infallibility resting with the world, "the way things are" — Teilhard, at points of specific conflict, did not always hold to this intention. Loyalty to Revelation, the unconscious desire to remain ultimately "orthodox", got in his way. Because of his personal spirituality, deeply ingrained in orthodoxy, either he was not always aware of the need to harmonize contradictions or, in his passionate desire to remain in his "divine milieu", the Society of Jesus, he chose to avoid confronting certain crucial issues, allowing his readers to make their own extrapolations and to draw their own conclusions.

Therefore, in very gratitude for the breakthrough Teilhard's vision has provided, and in loyalty to the Spirit that animated his great work, we are obliged to carry to their logical conclusion the directions of thought established in his pursuit of maximum coherence. Would it not, for example, be more consistent with Teilhard's vision of the "within" of cosmogenesis to reinterpret and understand the Incarnation as the flowering in Jesus of Nazareth of an incarnation, a Christ life, whose seed had been present in matter from the beginning of time? Teilhard nowhere questions the possibility, probability, or even appropriateness of a virgin birth in an evolving universe in which the peak of higher consciousness, even Christ-consciousness, is always present in seed form. To do so he would have had to distinguish between the Christ-life, or Christ consciousness, and the life of Jesus of Nazareth. Nowhere does he do this. Jesus and the Christ are for Teilhard always one reality, coterminous, identical. To have made a distinction, in my judgment, would have accorded better with the basic vision of unbroken continuity of development from within.

Happily he did not identify the process of salvation as dependent on Jesus' death upon the cross. There seems rather in Teilhard's view something akin to that of the

Fourth Gospel: "Greater love hath no man than this, that a man lay down his life for his friends" (John 15:13). The way of "complexity-consciousness" seems to be scientific terminology for "the royal way of the holy cross". He specifically rejects an emphasis in which "the cross is constantly held up before us to remind us of our world's initial miscarriage"[9] and insists "the Christian is not asked to swoon in the shadow, but to climb in the light, of the cross."[10] One would have thought he would have jumped to the conclusion that the process of salvation in evolutionary terms is the Christ-life in Jesus of Nazareth quickening and nourishing through active imagination the Christ-seed in every one of us. But he nowhere spells it out so simply, perhaps in unconscious loyalty to dogma.

Again, with reference to the doctrine of the resurrection, one wonders what place a flesh-and-bones resurrection has in an evolving universe? Teilhard nowhere denies the literal interpretation nor insists that the resurrection experiences must have been mystical in nature rather than physical, metaphorical rather than literal. We sense, once more, an unconscious desire not to provoke the authorities to a charge of heresy with the accompanying danger of at least posthumous excommunication. Would it not have been more consistent, more in accord with his own mystical proclivity, to interpret the experiences as mystical in nature, symbolic of the principle of the "survival of the fittest" in the evolutionary context? This kind of life is what lives and is, in fact, indestructible. It is in fact the Christ-life in Jesus that prompts Jesus' unforgettable words: "I am the resurrection and the life" (John 11:26).

Finally, one wonders whether it is consistent with the evolutionary perspective to forecast an omega point with such confidence, the "Christification" of the universe, or whether this may not be an unconscious projection from the Judaeo-Christian eschatological heritage upon a process that does not of itself speak of any end? Is this not an instance of what may be the human limitation, anthropomorphism? Teilhard would defend it on the ground of convergence, "tout ce qui mont converge" (everything that reaches up converges). This is understandable with reference to the spherical nature of the earth, but of the universe itself? One would be tempted to raise questions. Because we cannot envisage a moral and spiritual stage beyond that revealed in Jesus of Nazareth, does this mean that "Christification" of the universe will exhaust the potential of that mysterious seed within? Could that tree shrew which Loren Eiseley tells us once "contained" man have imagined the nature of his progeny? We can perceive with Teilhard the direction of evolution toward higher consciousness and more profound amorization. But are we in position to predict a denouement beyond which there is no new thing under our sun or any other suns? Clearly the next step is raised consciousness in the form of mystical or contemplative consciousness, Christ-consciousness. One step is enough for me. We cannot prophesy the distant scene.

But let not our critique detract from the basic contribution of Teilhard which has been to provide us with a great new myth of continuing creation within which everything else must be assimilated. He has provided a new framework within which to place all else, a master picture which enables us to put all the pieces of the jig-saw puzzle together. The evolution of life on this planet, once begun, *is a fact*, scientifically demonstrable on the basis of incontrovertible evidence recorded by the fossil remains in the earth's strata. Teilhard's vision of the vast enlargement of the evolutionary process on a cosmic scale is not a demonstrable fact because no scientific experiment can be designed to prove or disprove it. But it is an hypothesis so persuasive that "once to have known it, nothing else will do." The detailed elaboration of the hypothesis goes forward under many disciplines and may not be complete for generations.

APPLICATION OF THE VISION
TO SPIRITUAL GUIDANCE

What we are concerned with specifically here is the way this new perspective affects spiritual guidance. How does it illuminate the fact of spiritual guidance? How can the lines of spiritual guidance be brought into conformity with this curve?

To begin with, the only form of spiritual guidance which can be viable in the future is one which assimilates, or, more accurately, can be assimilated into, this vision or myth of cosmogenesis. The universe through the process of evolution is moving toward the incarnation of ever higher consciousness, making possible more profound spirituality. It is spirituality all the way down into the heart of matter and all the way up into the realized Christ-life and beyond. Spiritual guidance, in the light of this new conception of the world and its destination, must conform to the vast axis of complexity-consciousness on its proper course in humankind in order to preclude extinction and to further the purpose of evolution. We can speak for the first time now, as Thomas Berry has demonstrated, of a "spirituality of the earth", not one directed to the earth, but one emerging out of the very heart of the earth itself, a spirituality of the earth.

Basic religious education should involve an immersion in the study of evolution and particularly of its unfolding on a cosmic scale in the Teilhardian myth. We are to follow with Teilhard the lines passed by evolution until they achieve their maximum coherence. This is to train the eye to see, as Teilhard saw, the progressive flowering of the "within" of matter in consciousness and in spirit. What we begin to perceive is a great convergence of Jung's myth of the psyche and Teilhard's myth of cosmogenesis. The macrocosm of a cosmos still being born has its counterpart in the microcosm of a human being assimilating into wholeness its ever-changing and enlarging experiences, relationships, insights, while making conscious and integrating the contents of the unconscious. The counterpart of the vast universal theme of complexity-consciousness is the solitary process of individuation in each human person. For both the species as a whole and solitary human beings one demand remains constant: assimilate or perish (or cease to grow which in an evolving universe is one way to perish).

We can now begin to see what this new perspective means for spiritual guidance. It means that spiritual guides must be consciously evolving individuals who are concerned to help others catch the vision of an evolving universe and how it relates to the present direction of their solitary inward journey. It is to remain "on thread" oneself in this specific sense and to help others find their thread and to impart a procedure by which they can become conscious of staying on it, weaving their way forward in accordance with it. See, in this new light, how much we have going for us! Think of the momentum of the tidal wave of energy accumulated in this age-old process. As the body knows what it wants because of its very nature, if we can learn to communicate with the Self of our self in our own psyche, we shall come to know what it wants. John Donne has said with telling terseness, "the body is the book." So in an even larger sense "the psyche is the book" written on its inward parts by evolution itself, containing its own secret codes and revelations about its purpose and ultimate destination. We need to become attentive to and learn how to read this book.

In a process characterized at its center by a mysterious "within" which is endlessly producing new forms of life and consciousness, we need to become aware of our own "within", the mysterious depths of our own unconscious, to read our own edition of the great book of life, and to meditate on its laws day and night. Therefore self-knowledge in the Jungian sense of making conscious the contents of the unconscious and integrating those contents with consciousness becomes part of basic religious education. Religion is that instinct which motivates us to bind into one sheaf all that we now are and assigns us an unending work whose depth is illimitable, unfathomable.

At the Teilhard-Jung Symposium in 1975 in New York, it was said by one of the speakers that man is "the ecstatic mode of the earth". That is, in man, insofar as men and women experience ecstasy, it is the earth experiencing ecstasy for the first time. Insofar as men and women pray, the earth itself is at prayer for the first time. This is what we mean by the spirituality of the earth. Of course all this requires and produces a new respect, a new reverence for the earth, our mother in whose womb we were conceived, who gave us birth, and on whose bosom we are still nourished. The new science of ecology is given its *raison d'être* and is revealed as in operation on a cosmic scale in the interdependence of all life and all things. We have come into a way of seeing the earth as "good" that no previous generation has been afforded. Spiritual guidance, far from being a way to direct us out of an alien environment to an ultimate escape through death to some pleasanter world beyond, will now be concerned to help others relate to the good earth as the mother she is and to relate to all other creatures as the brothers and sisters they are. It is but one family with many branches. And the resources of the earth are to be used with consummate stewardship for they are a legacy our mother has bestowed upon us and the supply is limited.

Spiritual guidance becomes not the means by which I attain a heaven hereafter, but the means primarily to make me an appreciative and obedient child of this earth. As Teilhard expressed it in an epigrammatic way of deceptive simplicity, "All you have to do is hear the heart of the earth beating within you." That is one metaphor for "reading the book". I am to align my process of individuation with evolution's process of complexity consciousness. In this way I become not only a co-creator with God with reference to my own brief life but also cooperate with God's continuing creation within the human species. In some mysterious way, as we have tried to interpret, the human species is not only what it is at present, but also is a conduit for life that is intended still further to evolve. There remains a "within" at the mysterious depths of our being which contains the promise of a life form not yet incarnate on this earth. Now and again momentarily we catch glimpses of it. But we will recollect that "heaven gives its glimpses only to those not in position to look too close." Nevertheless we can see the next step: the higher consciousness emerging out of a disciplined cultivation of the mystical or contemplative faculty.

VALUES APPROPRIATE TO SPIRITUAL GUIDANCE

In *The New Story* Thomas Berry asks what the values are that characterize evolution itself on the assumption that if we could ascertain what these are we should have some standards to apply to our own personal lives. Berry identifies three factors in the evolutionary process that offer us clues as to what human behavior and values might be in harmony with the objectives of evolution. The first of these is differentiation. It seems that evolution apparently works toward differentiation. The proliferation of species from a single phylum is testimony to this built-in, functional pattern. Within the species the individual has also a tendency to develop toward differentiation, even from other members of the species. "Directed chance" takes this form in its groping toward the production of emergent mutations, sports, the basis of another species, perhaps the peduncle of a new phylum. This tendency toward differentiation is particularly visible and noticeable in the human species. Practiced consciously, this value becomes the quest of individuation.

This would be one of the first concerns of spiritual guidance in this contemporary mode. The counselee must be encouraged to be ever conscious of the process of differentiation, differentiation from one's peers, family, spouse, even one's role model, one's mentors and one's spiritual guide himself/herself. It is helpful to keep in mind here that the momentum of evolution itself provides both motivation and energy for differentiation. When one is going *with* this current, one must learn to give an account of the faith that is in one, to make one's own synthesis, even to insist on taking the creed metaphorically rather than literally, and to work out what one means by the metaphors and how one applies them in understanding the basic dynamics of life. Teilhard is a great example here. He was a superb "apologist" (interpreter, advocate) for the faith in the light of the unsettling doubts that clustered about the new evolutionary perspective. But while Teilhard can be enormously stimulating, his synthesis can not be taken over in its entirety by any believer who wants a first hand faith, as already suggested.

The guide must help the counselee to distinguish the conscience which is formed by what Freud called the super-ego in response to the mores and precepts of culture, church, society, etc., and the moral law discerned inwardly. The counselee may sometimes be called to stand against culture, his own community, his own church in loyalty to his or her own vision and perception. Jung speaks of the importance of every individual having a "secret" which she or he imparts to no one. The secret apparently is too intimate to articulate. It relates to the daimon within, what one values and feels called to do and to become, who one understands oneself to be at the core. When one has a secret and yields to the discernment of an imperious daimon one begins to fathom what differentiation is. One knows that one is on the road to individuation.

The second value of evolution which Thomas Berry isolates and identifies is interiority or subjectivity. It is not enough to be different from others. One must embark on the inward journey, to go deep within, to become familiar with the "feel" of one's own center. This relates to Teilhard's notion of the "within" of things and how this "within" intensifies with, and is heightened by, raised consciousness. The higher the evolved state, the more refined, energized, and pregnant with power becomes the "within". It is from this "within" that new birth and new growth takes place. Hence it is important to cultivate this inwardness of being, this interiority or subjectivity. Kierkegaard expressed it this way: "Are you always conscious of being an individual? Even in that most intimate of relationships, marriage, are you always conscious of that still more intimate relationship you bear to yourself as an individual before God?"[11] In the cultivation of interiority or subjectivity one learns to be on two levels at once. One develops a sense of the self and consciously relates what is happening and what one is thinking to the growing edge of the individuation process within. Feeling for the center is a way of keeping on thread and of exercising the mystical or contemplative faculty by consciously recollecting the presence of the God within, God in other persons, and God in the world. Relating to God within and to the center of one's own self is one movement of the Spirit.

The human being is a reflective, meditating, contemplating, that is to say, a praying animal. These activities, when they are performed in conscious companionship with or directed toward the God within, are the way the human being grows in interiority or subjectivity. This is the way a person deliberately enriches the quotient of the "within" with which she or he has been endowed and it is this "within" that bears the seed of further growth for that individual and for the species.

So the spiritual guide will be faithful in the discipline of prayer, of meditation, and of contemplation, and encourage her or his counselees in the practice of these disciplines. To become a spiritual guide, we will say again, is to become a developed mystic, a contemplative. We have learned from evolution that it is when the "within" is differentiated through an advance in complexity-consciousness that the stage is set for the next step forward in the particular line of evolution. Should it be different with regard to the human species? We know what the next step of raised consciousness is for us: mystical or contemplative consciousness.

The third value characteristic of evolution is communion. Differentiation first, interiority second, communion third. It is the intensity of differentiation and the depth of interiority that make meaningful and fruitful communion possible. This is what Teilhard calls "radial" meeting, from center to center, as distinct from tangential meeting. Genuine communion as distinct from superficial meeting is directly dependent on the quality and clarity of interiority. The deeper the interiority, the more profound the communion. And communion is not dependent on verbal exchange. Thomas Merton writes of the wordless communion of Trappist monks as they keep their silence and go about their several appointed tasks. Members of the Society of Friends have experienced in the silence of the

Quaker Meeting for Worship what they choose to call "communion after the manner of Friends".

Douglas Steere writes of that still deeper communion that awaits the cessation of talk between friends, no matter how close they had come through verbal communication. Martin Buber held that all real life is meeting. And the richest meeting is communion. Perhaps the meaning of life is most profoundly experienced in communion: communion with God and with one another, communion with God in one another. This must be what George Fox was talking about when he counseled Friends "to go cheerfully over the face of the earth, answering to that of God in everyone". Fenelon reminds us that "to hear the voice of the voiceless one must be silent before him."

A good measure of solitude and disciplined silence is essential to spiritual guides. It is from this interior posture that real communion can spring. A "meeting for spiritual guidance" must be an occasion for communion if it is to realize its full potential.

Differentiation, interiority, communion — the values emerging out of evolution itself — are the touchstones of effective spiritual guidance.

CHAPTER 4

SEXUALITY AND SPIRITUALITY

In the ministry of spiritual guidance, as in all other forms of counseling, one of the most important concerns is the creative integration of sexual energy. In every relationship there is a sexual component, however subtle and unrecognized. Freud did us a great service in demonstrating the omnipresence and pervasive importance of the sexual factor. We do not need to follow him in his conclusion that it is the most important single factor in human personality and in some aberrant form at the root of all neuroses to acknowledge that if we attach primary importance to the attainment of wholeness we dare not leave out of our account this potent element in the human psyche. The secular therapist is quite right to pose as an early question to his or her clients: "What are you currently doing with your sexuality?" The spiritual guide should be equally concerned about the quality of expression this energy finds in the counselee, though he or she may wait longer to pose the question, and find it still more important to ask, "What are you currently doing with your adoration quotient?"

No one of the current revolutions is of more crucial

significance to spiritual guidance than the so-called sexual revolution. The counselee is a sexual being as well as a spiritual being and it is very important for the spiritual guide to remain aware of this fact, to encourage candor and frank discussion in this area, and to be possessed of strong convictions and inner clarity regarding his or her own values here. Not that these values are to be imposed upon the counselee but, insofar as they can be shown to transcend cultural mores and warrant universal application, it is the guide's responsibility to interpret them and to explore with the counselee the way they might find expression in her or his individual life. As we shall presently see, I believe these values are rooted and grounded in evolution itself and confirmed by the findings of the depth psychology of C.G. Jung. Apart from hunger and thirst, the need for shelter and clothing, and the religious instinct to bind everything in one sheaf, the sexual drive is the most potent force in the human psyche. It is operative even when we are totally unaware of its presence. It can initiate and take over as an autonomous complex so imperious as to become a pretender to the inner throne of identity. On the other hand, this energy can serve to motivate growth in the life of the Spirit, as both Teilhard and Jung testified. In any case spiritual guidance has to do with the whole person and one cannot afford to neglect the proper assimilation of this powerful drive which can be directed to good or ill. We therefore do well to try to understand this energy in the psyche and to ask what values it is to serve.

There has presently been enough of the diffuse and amorphous counsel that we must be compassionate and understanding, nonjudgmental and accepting of different sexual lifestyles. Beginning with the pace-setting and courageous "Toward a Quaker View of Sex" by a very professional and competent group of British Quakers, there has been much laboring with the concern to eradicate prejudice, to assure justice, and to open minds toward the possibility of new values emerging from the current sexual experimentation. Much of this concern I celebrate as not only valid but essential if we are to outgrow the darker aspects of our puritan heritage. But where are we being offered moral insight or spiritual uplift in this area? Is there, indeed, among the great range of ways, or sexual lifestyles, a more excellent way? This is a question a spiritual guide must inevitably ask.

THE NEED FOR A NEW MYTHOLOGY

The time has come, I believe, to expend energy and passion in the quest of a new sexual morality with fixed reference points, disciplines, aspirations. This is an issue about which we can no longer turn to the Bible for the definitive word that will speak with authority to our contemporary world. The authors of the Bible defend a fairly consistent sexual morality, but on the basis of a mythology that is no longer relevant for us, having to do with lost innocence in a Garden of Eden, the psalmist's lament "in sin hath my mother conceived me," and a body-spirit dichotomy characteristic of many passages in the New Testament. Some of the attitudes toward various forms of sexuality in the Bible strike many of our contemporaries as little more than primitive taboos without adequate rational support.

It is true that these taboos may have arisen as social prohibitions without a carefully worked-out, conscious rationale. But even when taboos emerge for reasons that later become unacceptable or for no plausible, stated reasons at all, this does not necessarily mean that the society which practiced them was not intuitively on the right track as revealed by subsequent insight and wisdom. It is sometimes possible in life to discover that one has been doing the right thing for the wrong reasons. It may be that under the aegis of a new mythology that speaks to the condition of our time, and fresh revelation concerning the origin and destiny of humankind, we shall find much of the Biblical morality reinstated as still valid.

As we said, however, we can no longer accept on Biblical authority a sexual morality for today. The death of the Biblical mythology of sex and the comparative safety and effectiveness of the new contraceptives have together produced the contemporary sexual revolution. It is my strong conviction that only a viable new mythology is capable of providing and motivating a new sexual morality. I believe that the lineaments of such a relevant new mythology have emerged and are beginning to coalesce as the result of the seminal thinking and intuitive insights of the two great contemporary minds and spirits to whom we have been turning for prophetic insight: Teilhard de Chardin and C. G. Jung.

This new mythology to which I refer arises naturally, not in a forced or artificial way, from new perspectives on the nature of humankind that have so recently become available to us through the independent research and reflection of these two scientists and mystics, Teilhard and Jung. It is characteristic of a mythology that it either does or does not speak to the condition of an individual. If it does, then it has a curious way of seizing and shaping that individual's very being, influencing values and dictating commitments. Increasing numbers of men and women are finding these compatible mythologies merging into one, or at any rate converging, and are also finding that both on conscious and unconscious levels they are giving interior consent, responding with a reverberating "yea". This convergence of conviction is impressive and relevant to the kind of spiritual guidance we are advocating.

THE RELATIONSHIP BETWEEN SEX AND SPIRIT

We ask, now, are there any guidelines that the spirituality we have been proposing would impose on the exercise of one's sexuality? Although sexuality may be the best word we can find to symbolize the enormous energy that is deeply rooted in human beings relating to the reproductive function, I prefer to use here the shorthand symbol "sex" as suggesting something a little more concrete and in touch with the vernacular. In place of "spirituality", I prefer to speak of "Spirit" and invoke from our heritage all the numinous overtones that have been associated with the phrase "Holy Spirit". Let "sex" then for our present purpose refer to the instinct and energy (libido) in human beings that prompts to all manner of manifestations, whether overt or in fantasy, not limited to reproductive intent, however rooted biologically in that function.

By "Spirit" I am going to mean something quite specific. The connotations of this word can be so elusive as to evaporate altogether. However suspect Paul's understanding of sex may have been both theologically and psychologically, his attempt to delineate the marks of the Spirit have not been surpassed. He who could sing the paean of praise to love in the thirteenth chapter of First Corinthians can be entrusted with the privilege of defining Spirit for us. As with the highest form of human love, he described Spirit for us by isolating and identifying its fruits: "The harvest of the Spirit is love, joy, peace, patience, kindness, goodness, fidelity, gentleness, and self-control" (Gal. 5:22). However elusive the definition of Spirit may be, I am prepared for the purposes of this inquiry to accept these specific manifestations as eloquently attesting its presence in men and women. Let us state them again: love, joy, peace, patience, kindness, goodness, fidelity, gentleness, and self-control. Now, do these characteristics bear any relationship to the whole gamut of sexual expression?

There is abroad in our contemporary world an apparently growing point of view that insists there is no more relationship between sex and Spirit than between eating and Spirit (though even here, in a profound sense, there may be relationship). It is suggested that both are merely physical appetites whose assuagement is a matter of individual choice. Of course, the value of the health of the body imposes limitations in both areas. And those expressions of sex which involve other persons must preclude any form of violence. This much is conceded. But no other moral or spiritual dictum is acceptable for those who approach the problem in this way.

If we are to be attentive presently to the new

mythological framework which Teilhard has offered us for this whole question it may be well to recognize how clearly he heard the extent of the detachment many of our contemporaries have made between sex and Spirit. In any controversy, the test of competence is the capacity to articulate the adversary's point of view as well as he does himself so that he knows you have heard him. So Teilhard, in building his case in an extraordinary essay entitled "The Evolution of Chastity", first puts the position of the radical opposition in these words:

> 'In short, we often hear, sexuality has no significance at all from the moral and religious point of view: you might as well speak of running your digestion on moral principles. So far as the sexual side is concerned, man must no doubt have a care for health, and exercise temperance. A controlled use will give him balance and an added zest for action. But by no stretch of imagination can we agree that physical chastity has anything to do with spiritual virtue. There is no direct relationship between sanctity and sexuality.'[12]

Then Teilhard proceeds to develop his own central thesis: there is indeed a very direct relationship between sanctity and sexuality, or, as I am putting it, between Spirit and sex. We might have drawn an intimation of this from what I take to be a very common experience. Have you not in corporate worship or in prayer in solitude on occasion found sensual fantasy persistently intruding upon spiritual reverie? Have you not found these curiously inseparable companions an interior embarrassment if not an occasion for debilitating guilt? Now if you can report in all honesty that this is never your experience I am forced to concede that yours is an "innocence" I have not known. Another plausible explanation of my "aberration" of course is that in my childhood and youth I repressed more sexual energy than you and that it is now overtaking me from the unconscious when my idling conscious mind gives it opportunity.

But I suspect that this phenomenon, though not as yet explored as far as I am aware by Kinsey's relentless research, is almost universal. Certainly it was not foreign to Anthony in the desert, nor Augustine in Carthage. Literature attests it all the way from Erskine Caldwell's portrayal of the retarded boy masturbating and reciting the Lord's Prayer simultaneously in *Tobacco Road* to Dante's energy in storming the very gates of heaven, driven by his sublimated love for Beatrice, in the *Divine Comedy*. A close observation of this human proclivity might have made us suspect all along the direct relationship between sex and Spirit, despite the overwhelming weight of our conditioning to the contrary. These unwelcome intrusions in worship, indicating unfinished, even as yet unaccepted, business from the unconscious, must be given attention if real spiritual progress is to be made. Is this not one of the *coniunctio oppositorum* (conjunction of opposites), in Jungian terms, that I am to realize if I am to keep moving ahead along the royal path of individuation, wholeness or holiness of life? My answer would be in the affirmative.

And is there not a strange similarity between the altered state of consciousness in orgasm, a kind of transcendence of personality, and classic mystical experience? Does the sexual counterpart presage the spiritual? Does the ancient practice of providing temple prostitutes reflect a perversion of a potential realized in the sexual union of those in whom the marks of the Spirit support and accompany lovemaking?

Human beings are animals. We are no longer able to picture ourselves as standing apart from the animal kingdom. Remy de Gourmont is indisputably right when he asserts: "There is no gulf between man and the animals...we are animals....When we make love, we truly do so, to use the theologian's phrase, *more bestiarum*, like the beasts. Love is deeply animal."[13]

And Teilhard, from a different perspective, cries Alleluiah! Just so! He is fully conscious of the uninterrupted continuity between animal sexuality and spirituality in the human animal. Pierre Burney, a secular ethicist who understands Teilhard's position remarkably well, in undertaking to interpret it, quotes from Jean Rostand:

Whether one likes it or not, whatever ideas one upholds, the whole fabric of human love, with all the animality and the sublimation the word implies, with its frenzy and its self-sacrifice, and with all its lightness of touch, its pathos and its terrors, is yet built up on the minute molecular variations of a few compounds of phenanthrene. Does this take all the poetry out of love?

Then Burney interjects, "Here Rostand has reached the nadir of materialist reduction," but abruptly he reverses the process with this profound saying: "Does this take all the poetry out of love? What if it fills chemistry with poetry?"[14] He is quite right. We do not have to resort, like Kinsey, to a reduction from the higher to the lower. It is still open to us, like Teilhard, to perceive in the lower the veiled promise of the higher.

TEILHARD'S MYTH OF MATTER AND SPIRIT

The new myth, in flat contradiction of the inherited myth, finds no dichotomy between matter and Spirit. As life sprang from matter in the evolution of this planet, so Spirit has emerged from life. In the process of evolution the earth has literally grown humankind. There was no fall from grace in a mythical Garden of Eden. Indeed there was no Garden of Eden, nor any one first man or first woman. Our species emerged imperceptibly from its forebears. The dawn of self-consciousness, reflection, and moral perception was gradual, at the patient pace of evolution. Eating of the fruit of the tree of the knowledge of good and evil may be retained as a metaphor to represent the rise of moral perception, but it must now be related not to a Fall but to a quantum leap forward.

In the Teilhardian mythology of continuing creation, as distinct from a fixed cosmology, the central concept, as we have seen, is the unbroken continuity between pre-life and life and between life and reflection. As life lay asleep as a seed in matter, so Spirit indwelt life from the most primitive forms upward. Indeed, from this perspective Spirit emerged directly from matter through the agency of life. Spirit, like life, is the "within" of matter. If we are to understand the further development of Teilhard's mythology with reference to sex and Spirit, we must remember this notion of everything developing gradually in the context of biological space-time from apparently inanimate matter to the highest expression of Spirit. The operating law of this vast movement is one of complexity-consciousness. The whole history of this planet reflects from the beginning a tendency in matter to produce life under just the right ecological conditions and the tendency in life to move in the direction of higher forms of consciousness until Spirit becomes manifest, once again in unbroken continuity. This is the very axis along which the whole process of evolution moves. Humankind is the arrowhead indicating presently the farthest up-reach, the vanguard on this planet in this noble procession to higher forms of consciousness.

Let me suggest a playful image that may help to impart this idea to those unfamiliar with it. The story goes that a woman, in conversing with her psychiatrist, informed him that she knew what held up the universe. In response to his interested query she divulged the secret: "a turtle". Instinctively pressing the question to a deeper level, in typical psychoanalytical style, he asked what upheld the turtle, to which the woman replied, undaunted, "another turtle". Quite unchanged in expression, despite the extraordinary revelation, and hoping to produce a confrontation with the unconscious by nonplussing the woman, he asked quietly, "But what is holding up that second turtle?" Then the woman smiled a wonderful smile of utter confidence, blended with a gentle compassion for the doctor's unfortunate ignorance, and said: "Doctor, it's turtles all the way down." Jung would not have failed to notice that the turtle is an archetypal image emerging from the collective unconscious in various mythologies for the obvious reason, perhaps, that only the turtle has a back strong enough proportionately to support the universe.

Now what Teilhard is saying may strike us initially as an equally mad form of hallucination. But to all who can hear him he is imparting a new revelation: it's Spirit all the way down from the peak of its manifestations in human beings to the very heart of the most primitive forms of matter. This is the "diaphany of the Divine at the heart of the universe on fire" of which his recurring mystical experience speaks. Charged by the authorities with the heresy of pantheism for this teaching, Teilhard insisted that he was not saying that matter was God, but rather that God shone through matter in a luminous way from within. This position would be not pantheism, as Teilhard explained, but pan-entheism: not God as matter but God at the heart of matter. The idea of continuing creation, of the essential goodness of matter as Spirit-laden, and of the up-reach of Spirit through matter, is indeed a myth. But religion has never known how to speak of the ultimate truth which it believes it has perceived save through myth and metaphor.

This myth, Teilhard insists, is simply a new way of "seeing" our universe. We cannot prove its literal truth, as we have earlier acknowledged. But the same thing may be said of the older myth of a finished creation and the origin of human evil through original sin in the Garden of Eden. The difference is that the older myth no longer fits the fact of the evolution of life on this planet from more primitive forms. This fact constitutes fresh revelation in the last century. The new myth, an insight arising from the unconscious of one man, is increasingly confirmed as compatible with current scientific observations and individual experiences, both conscious and unconscious.

THE IMPLICATIONS OF THE NEW MYTH

We recognize that the older myth of the Fall has been responsible for the two traditional injunctions of the Catholic Church: that the union of the sexes is good, even holy, but only when the conscious intent is procreation within marriage, and second, that apart from this express purpose and context any intimacy between the sexes must be reduced to a minimum. We note, however, that Vatican II has since conceded that intercourse within marriage is good, whether or not procreation is intended. Moreover, the Catholic Church has held that the state of virginity involves an even higher moral ideal than marriage. What has produced the Christian cult of chastity in this traditional sense? Teilhard responds that in the first place there has been a physiological presupposition that "sexual relations are tainted by some degradation or defilement." He goes on to explain the assumptions behind the Church's earlier position in his essay, "The Evolution of Chastity":

> By the material conditions of its act, by the physical transports it entails, by a sort of clouding of the personality that accompanies it — 'passion,' man instinctively feels, has something about it of animality, of shame, of fever, of stupefaction, of fear, of mystery. Here we meet, in its most basic and most insistent form, and at its most acute, the whole intellectual and moral problem of matter. Sexuality is sinful.[15]

Society's fear of contamination and the guilt attached to encouraging wrongdoing gave rise to a whole system of restrictive asceticism in relation to sexual practice.

> To avoid any risk of vertigo, one has to stay as far as possible on the safe side of the cliff — one has to run away. In order not to give way to the blandishments of pleasure, in order not to be carried away by enjoyment, one has to cut away the very roots of pleasure and inflict pain on oneself: privation and penance. . . . However — and this is to the credit of the gospel — this asceticism is justified for Christians only insofar as it develops ultimately into a refined mysticism.[16]

Teilhard describes this mysticism in the traditional metaphor of becoming the bride of Christ and suggests that Christian chastity is ultimately a "transposition into religion of the lover's fidelity".[17] True Christianity has never altogether condemned matter as did the Gnostic heretics. Witness sacramental practices and the very hope of a resurrection! Yet this care for the body is confused with an odd mistrust of the earth's resources.

> Creatures are good; and yet they are not good. The world might well have been created as we see it and yet it contains within itself a hidden perversion. And so once more we come up against the complexity of the still insufficiently intellectualized notion of the original Fall.[18]

To this inherited predeliction, Teilhard opposes his new perception:

> Spiritual ramifications have their roots deep in the corporeal. It is from man's storehouse of passion that the warmth and light of his soul arise, transfigured. It is there, initially, that we hold concentrated, as in a seed, the finest essence, the most delicately adjusted spring, governing all spiritual development.
> When we have finally weighed things up, it is apparent that only Spirit is worth our pursuit; but deep within us there exists a system of linkages, both sensitive and profound, between Spirit and matter.[19]

So Teilhard insists that "underlying the religion (or moral science) of Spirit, a new moral conception of matter is asserting itself."[20] This new perception of the universe proposes that Spirit universally emerges through matter, including sexuality. Teilhard perceives, moreover, that the spirituality of the future will be based on the dyad, on that man and woman in relationship whose union is "richer" and "more spiritualizing" than union for the sake of procreation alone.

> It is not in isolation (whether married or unmarried), but in paired units, that the two portions, masculine and feminine, of nature are to

rise up towards God. The view has been put forward that there can be no sexes in spirit. This arises from not having understood that their duality was to be found again in the composition of divinized being. After all, however 'sublimated' man may be imagined to be, he certainly is not a eunuch. Spirituality does not come down upon a 'monad' but upon the human 'dyad'.[21]

Then he arrives at his conclusion regarding the criteria for a new sex ethic:

It used to be urged that the natural manifestations of love should be reduced as much as possible. We now see that the real problem is how to harness the energy they represent and transform them. We must not cut down on them, but go beyond them. Such will be our new ideal of chastity . . . . Rightly speaking, there are no sacred or profane things, no pure or impure: there is only a good direction and a bad direction — the direction of ascent, of amplifying unity, of greatest spiritual effort; and the direction of descent, of constricting egoism, of materializing enjoyment. If they are followed in the direction which leads upward, all creatures are luminous; if grasped in the direction which leads downward, they lose their radiance and become, we might almost say, diabolical. According to the skill with which we set our sails to their breeze, it will either capsize our vessel or send it leaping ahead.[22]

What Teilhard seems to be saying is that Spirit extends all the way down in ever more primitive forms into animal sexuality and below into the source of life in matter. But if it is Spirit all the way down into animal sexuality and below, the inevitable and irrevocable corollary is that it is sex all the way up into the highest reaches of Spirit achieved by humankind and beyond. In our terms sex is the channel through which the ascent of the Spirit has primarily taken place in animals, reaching its current peak in the animal, humankind. The process by which Spirit rises through sex is one of sublimation. The marks of the Spirit which Paul so effectively identified — love, joy, peace, patience, kindness, goodness, fidelity, gentleness, and self-control — become then the names for the various forms which the sublimation must take if sex in the individual is to be a channel for continued growth in the life of the Spirit. What is of supreme importance is the direction in which Spirit is moving in the sexual expression of an individual — that is, whether it is moving retrogressively toward more primitive animality or toward more sublimated hominization. Here is the touchstone for spiritual guidance in this critical area.

When, however, toward the close of his essay "The Evolution of Chastity," Teilhard returns to the theme that physical chastity or celibacy brings with it a sort of "absolute superiority" and that some "perfection resides in virginity by *nature*", I think his development of the idea goes awry. In that essay Teilhard refers to the heroine of a Russian novel (which he does not name) as expressing the idea that "We shall in the end find another way of loving." A spiritual fecundity will apparently supercede material fecundity. "Union for the sake of the child — but why not union for the sake of the work, for the sake of the idea?"[23] he asks. Then he suggests that "this spiritual use of the flesh [is] precisely what many men of genius, men who have been true creators, have instinctively found and adopted."[24] I think he is speaking autobiographically here as well. Elsewhere he confides that he had never achieved a synthesis of thought except in dialogue with a woman. Another essay bears the significant title "The Feminine is the Unitive". But one suspects that he was under unconscious constraint to defend virginity as somehow a superior vocation because of his deep identification with the monastic ethos.

I do not accept vocational virginity or celibacy as a superior moral or spiritual attainment. Nor do I feel that Teilhard's position here is fully consistent with the general trend of his thinking or the substance of the myth he interprets for us. That matter is consummated by Spirit I can understand and affirm. That Spirit can ever on this earth disengage itself wholly from matter I have not experienced (save perhaps in the intimations of the immortality of a loved one) and therefore cannot accept. While I cannot embrace the proposition that "virginity rests upon chastity as thought upon life", I can accept his conclusion: "It is biologically evident that to gain control of passion and so make it serve Spirit must be a condition of progress."[25]

Perhaps it might be said that all profound love of two persons for one another requires an accompanying virginity with reference to relationship to others outside the dyad, and ultimately to a creative acceptance of a form of virginity with reference to each other imposed by advanced old age, as part of a new, deepening love for each other. Certainly I exult in the superb vision with which Teilhard brings to a close his essay on "The Evolution of Chastity":

> "The day will come when, after harnessing the ether, the winds, the tides, gravitation, we shall harness for God the energies of love. And, on that day, for the second time in the history of the world man will have discovered fire."[26]

One of the abiding insights of Freud was that civilization has been built on the repression of sex. What he meant was that the energy that might have gone into overt sexual expression was thereby conserved and channeled into the constructive building of human institutions. Teilhard, in like manner, laments the enormous waste of energy in a single day and night around the world in sexual expression that is not harnessed to the Spirit. I am sure he would have agreed that much lovemaking, quite apart from intent for procreation, can further the growth of the individual and deepen the communion between the dyad. What he is condemning is detached sexuality which is not building deeper relatedness and furthering growth in the life of the Spirit. At a time when we have become very conscious of the need to conserve the energy resources of the earth it is important to reflect also on the conservation of human energy and its dedication to the advance of Spirit in humankind.

JUNG'S EXTENSION OF THE MYTH

If Teilhard took within his purview the whole of cosmogenesis, C. G. Jung focused his attention upon the evolution of the human psyche within historic times. It is interesting that at the time of his death an open copy of *The Phenomenon of Man* was found on Jung's desk. Meantime, Teilhard had spoken approvingly of the insights of Jung and in the essay to which we referred he says that "the most important basis of psychoanalysis is that the energy which fuels our interior life and determines its fabric is in its primitive roots of a passionate nature." He recognized the importance of depth psychology in the continuing study of the phenomenon of man. Though these two men did not know one another personally, they were on convergent courses and the seminal thinking of both meet and mutually stimulate one another within the minds of those who are students of both. It is not surprising that the C. G. Jung Foundation and the American Teilhard Association collaborated on the one hundredth anniversary of Jung's birth and the twentieth anniversary of Teilhard's death in 1975 in holding a Jung-Teilhard Symposium, in New York City, an auspicious beginning of a dialogue, pursued vicariously and posthumously on their behalf by their followers, that will continue into the future.

Jung was also the author of a new mythology. As with Teilhard, this new mythology emerged in him through dialogue with his unconscious. He expressly stated his belief that "the unconscious is the only accessible source of religious experience" and he summoned us to the integration of the unconscious and the conscious elements in our psyche, the process he identified as one of individuation. It involves, we recall, the *coniunctio oppositorum*, the conjunction of opposites, a creative unity realized through tension between the shadow and persona, masculine and feminine components within the personality, sex and Spirit. It is not that sex and Spirit are antithetical. It is that some overt expressions of sexual impulse and aspiration Spirit-ward are antithetical as men and women evolve. Specific sexual practices may constitute a backward or downward movement with reference to the evolutionary forward movement or ascent of Spirit — through sex.

Freud was the first to recognize the pervasiveness of sexual energy on all levels, conscious and unconscious, in the human psyche. This is fully consonant with the Teilhardian perspective and mythology. Jung did not quarrel with this basic perception. He protested only when Freud sought to relate every neurosis to a sexual source. That the erotic element, when it could be identified as involved in a given neurotic manifestation, was likely to be the most potent factor, he did not doubt. But the Adlerian drive toward power had also to be reckoned with. And above all the therapist had to be alert to what may have gone amiss in the quest by the psyche of its meaning, its "story", its identity. For Jung, this always bore relationship to a loss of faith, a disengagement from a viable mythology for those in mid-life and beyond.

That in some sense it was sex all the way up into the higher reaches of Spirit through individuation Jung also believed. In fact, the archetypes of the anima and animus represent in Jung an internalization of the external distinctions in sex. Part of the process of individuation, that which moves in the direction of integration, wholeness, or holiness of life is the realization of a kind of androgynous potential in the individual. It is an interior marriage of the masculine and feminine principles that alone makes possible profound psychic as well as physical marriage in the human dyad. Jung would not have approved the blurring of distinctions in the current view that differences are culturally conditioned and not inherent. One of his ablest interpreters and former patients, Jolande Jacobi, whose book, *Masks of the Soul*, has been published posthumously, expresses the concern that some in the feminist movement, insofar as they emphasize cultural conditioning exclusively, do a grave disservice to the movement:

> People are less and less willing to face the fact
> that God created the two sexes quite different, with

different wavelengths, different means of expressing themselves, and different ways of loving. It is easy to make snap judgments of others based on oneself, and woman's current drive for absolute equality with men shows that they think they can be like men if only they have the will for it. This, however, is simply not true. The basic difference cannot be eradicated, though it can be distorted, to the detriment of human relationships.[27]

At the same time she is quite prepared to concede, with the Jungian mythology she espoused:

... every human being is, to some extent, both a man and a woman. Every man carries his Eve within himself, and every woman her Adam. As a result of this duality we relate to each other not only through the sex we consciously belong to, but also transversely, through our unconscious, contrasexual sides.[28]

Within the Jungian context we can identify another way in which it is sex all the way up into Spirit, not only through the sexual element in every human relationship including the most fulfilling marriages and sublimated friendships, but also by reason of the masculine-feminine components within the individual. When a man and woman relate radially, in wholeness, from center to center, there is formed a living organic mandala in the mystery of the new creation, their union of in-between-ness. The more permanent the relationship, the more unconditional the commitment, the more exquisite the ultimate mandala, shaped by this foursquare interrelatedness between the man, his anima, the woman, and her animus. One lifetime is sometimes not long enough to ring all the changes on this carillon or to respond to all the permutations of this kaleidoscope. When this unlimited potential for union is explored within the framework demanded by Spirit what is experienced is holy marriage within each individual and with each other.

In the light of the potential for human growth through individuation with reference to this new mythology, all love between man and woman which is characterized by overt sexual expression but is not at the same time increasingly reflecting the marks of the Spirit must be seen as in some sense an arrested development. Granted there are enormous variations in the quality of given relationships, still, must not the current practice of open marriage in which one or both of the partners engage in extramarital sexual relationship be seen as representing an arrested development in the individual? And is not marriage in this case a reversion to a lower level of sex-informed and sex-inspired Spirit, a form not rising to the responsibilities involved in the realization of the human potential?

The current emphasis by some young idealists on "simplicity of life" is altogether admirable and a worthy successor to the earlier emphases on civil rights and peace education. One aspect of the new movement, however, gives me pause. There is an accompanying sexual experimentation and it is sometimes suggested that this is part of the witness. This seems to me altogether incongruous with the emphasis on simplicity of life. It rather introduces a form of complexity at a point where physical and psychological energies can be easily dispersed and wasted. Much present sexual experimentation, while it is sometimes temporarily accompanied by an exhilarating sense of liberation, may in reality lead to inward forms of unrecognized bondage, threatening both simplicity of life and genuine integrity, thereby constituting a form of arrested development. When there are multiple contemporary sexual relationships, they tend either to become casual and depersonalized, or, if depth of encounter is sought, tend to be wanting in integrity, since real depth cries out for singularity, shared sacrifice, and fidelity.

These marks of the Spirit to which I am holding as the best criteria for judging the quality of an overt sexual relationship apply to homosexual relationships as well. This means that many an individual homosexual union, judged by these standards, is far superior to many an individual heterosexual union. I have known homosexual marriages that reflect the harvest of the Spirit in high degree. It is for homosexuals to comment on how this mythology applies to their orientation, if they see it as relevant. But I feel I must point out that in the Jungian context of the new mythology I am advocating, the degree of individuation ultimately attainable is likely to be more limited, generally speaking, when the interior masculine and feminine components are drawn into lively response only by another of the same sex.

Moreover, the organic mandala made possible through the dynamic interaction between two persons of the same sex, while in given instances no doubt of a better quality than a given heterosexual relationship, cannot, by reason of its obvious limitation, generally attain the same richness of pattern, or so it seems to me. With reference to the full human potential and depending upon the capacity of the individual, homosexuality may also be seen as a form of arrested development, whatever the complex causes. Depending on the depth and permanence of the orientation, in given instances the homosexual relationship may represent the only context within which any real development can take place. But we do have a responsibility, I believe, assuming that all children and adults have a bisexual potential in varying degree, to encourage the heterosexual development, when this is possible, for the sake of greater individuation and, potentially, a still richer union with another human being of the opposite sex.

THE IDEAL OF INDIVIDUATION

Erich Neumann in *Amor and Psyche* has given us a superb Jungian understanding of the Greek myth concerning Eros and Psyche. Their lovemaking in the dark produced an animal paradise of sensuality. Eros wanted to keep the experience on this level. But Psyche was irresistibly drawn toward higher consciousness. She broke her promise to Eros that she would never attempt to see him in the light, that is, in the perspective of higher consciousness of Spirit. In so doing, though she temporarily alienated him and drove

him away, she embarked not only on her own individuation, her journey to integrate within the unconscious and
the conscious, but also became the occasion in him
ultimately for the same up-reach of Spirit. Psyche's journey
required that she pass arduous tests demanding creative use
and integration of her masculine component before she
could see Eros again. But the final test before reconciliation
with Eros was Psyche's recognition of relatedness and love
as the source of her deepest identity and individuation as
a woman. It is precisely her individuation, her fusion of sex
and Spirit, that wins her divinization and admission to the
pantheon of the gods. More than this, in her marriage of
heaven and earth she had shown herself superior to the
existing gods, establishing a new value as divine, one
Aphrodite herself had not achieved: a higher form of
consciousness that united body, mind and spirit, the
unconscious and the fruits of consciousness. Neumann puts
it this way:

> The embrace of Eros and Psyche in the darkness
> represents the elementary but unconscious attrac-
> tion of opposites, which impersonally bestows life
> but is not yet human. But the coming of light makes
> Eros 'visible,' it manifests the phenomenon 'of
> psychic love, hence of all human love, as the human
> and higher form of the archetype of relatedness. It
> is only the completion of Psyche's development,
> effected in the course of her search for the invisible
> Eros, that brings with it the highest manifestation
> of the archetype of relatedness: a divine Eros joined
> with a divine Psyche.
>   Psyche's individual love for Eros as love in the
> light is not only an essential element, it is *the*
> essential element in feminine individuation.
> Feminine individuation and the spiritual develop-
> ment of the feminine — and herein lies the basic
> significance of this myth — are always effected
> through love. Through Eros, through her love of
> him, Psyche develops not only toward him, but
> toward herself. . . . But the unique feature of
> Psyche's development is that she achieves her
> mission not directly but indirectly, that she

performs her labors with the help of the masculine, but not as a masculine being.[29]

It is interesting that we speak of the feminine soul of man but never of the masculine soul of woman. Psyche is the name for the soul in man and woman alike; in both it is feminine. In another place Neumann reflects:

> Psyche dissolves her *participation mystique* with her partner and flings herself and him into the destiny of separation that is consciousness. Love as an expression of feminine wholeness is not possible in the dark, as a merely unconscious process; an authentic encounter with another involves consciousness, hence also the aspect of suffering and separation. Psyche's act leads, then, to all the pain of individuation, in which a personality experiences itself in relation to a partner as something other, that is as not only connected with the partner. . . . With Psyche, then, there appears a new love principle, in which the encounter between the feminine and masculine is the basis of individuation.[30]

And this is to be understood both externally in the man-woman relationship and internally in the man-anima and woman-animus relationship. The ancient Greek myth, without use of Jungian terminology, supports as an independent source from the collective unconscious the dynamic which both the Teilhardian and Jungian mythologies articulate for us in contemporary terms. Sexuality in the human animal is to rise above the unconscious to the higher forms of consciousness, reflecting the marks of the Spirit. Psyche does not love Eros the less but infinitely more.

In the Greek myth Psyche's capacity to love Eros paradoxically grows stronger and more beautiful even as she experiences more "otherness" and individuation. It is not wider experience in overt lovemaking with others that produces the personal growth by Psyche and enables growth in her lover. Rather, it is her lifelong fidelity that simultaneously enriches the union and makes possible the more profound individuation of both. Teilhard, as we have recognized earlier, perceived the remarkable paradox in this kind of relatedness and identified in it the operation of a law: "union differentiates". So the Teilhardian insight into the development of Spirit and sex and the Jungian identification of the development of a new fruit of the Spirit, individuation, from the encounter of the masculine and feminine, externally and internally — in other words from sex — fit well together.

What does all this have to say about our current quest for the basis of a new sexual morality related to a more profound spirituality? First, it provides, I believe, a new and viable mythology which can motivate us in this personal and social quest, through fresh revelation about laws that are written by God upon our inward parts. We have referred to Teilhard's discovery of the law of complexity-consciousness by which Spirit emerges from matter through sexuality in the continuing evolutionary process. Ever higher forms of union and human relatedness are the present observable consequence of the operation of this law. Another law operative in human relationships emerging from the energy inherent in sex is designated, as we have seen, union differentiates. Jung recognized this as a facet of the process of individuation advanced by an abiding man-woman relationship. Its interior counterpart is integration by the man of his anima and the woman of her animus.

This mythology, growing as it does out of a new understanding of the human psyche, its source and destiny on this earth, supports, I believe, as a more excellent way, an enduring and sexually exclusive relationship between one man and one woman as most conducive to growth in the life of the Spirit for all who are not expressly called to the celibate life. This is not to deny that many such relationships, begun in good faith, are properly dissolved when they become mutually destructive. Nor is it to deny that homosexual relationships may provide the only sexual union open to many persons. We should support these unions when they further the life of the Spirit by the same criteria we apply to heterosexual union. Both heterosexual and homosexual marriages, whether legalized by civil or religious ceremony or not, if they are to meet the human potential for development in the life of the Spirit, will be increasingly characterized by love, joy, peace, patience, kindness, goodness, fidelity, gentleness, and self-control.

In an earlier chapter we talked about three values incarnate in evolution itself: differentiation, interiority, communion. It is not difficult to see how these apply to sexuality. That form of sexual expression and union is best which effectively differentiates, for real union differentiates. Again that form of union is good which fosters and encourages the interiority and subjectivity of both, thus furthering individuation and a marriage of the masculine and feminine components in each individual. Where differentiation and real interiority are present, more profound communion is possible, communion of which sexual intercourse is the sacrament, "the outward and visible sign of the inward and spiritual grace". Clearly these values are furthered most by an exclusive relationship, and one in which the mutual commitment is abiding and unconditional.

CHAPTER 5

CULTIVATING
THE GIFT FOR
SPIRITUAL
GUIDANCE

There are some important distinctions between spiritual guidance on the one hand and psychotherapy and other forms of therapy on the other. This is not to say that the individual therapist may not function as a spiritual guide in the individual instance if she or he has genuine reverence for the psyche of the client and is a profoundly religious person. But the very name, therapist, suggests that the objective is to help the client solve a particular problem or to be released from the symptoms of a particular neurosis. Generally this implies a problem-centered approach with the objective of adjustment, the ability to function better within the sphere of the client's relationships and responsibilities. This often involves a subtle and tacit acceptance of both the mores and the values of the social milieu in which the client is called to live and move and have his or her being.

Much of the current pastoral counseling may also be characterized in this way. "Pastoral" implies a connection with the Church and therefore with the Christ myth, but the connection is often tenuous and unclear. The focus of attention is on the problems brought by the client and their resolution or amelioration by psychological techniques. The process, as generally practiced, is not so much a ministry within the Christian ethos as it is a profession with a largely secular and eclectic orientation to psychological principles. The context in which the counseling takes place is not clearly defined and the world view or ultimate concern of the counselor is not considered of central importance. In practice this often means that what goes on in the pastoral counseling session does justice neither to the numinous element in religion nor to the scientific element in psychology.

THE SCOPE OF SPIRITUAL GUIDANCE

The objective of spiritual guidance, on the other hand, is to serve as a means by which the consultee may be guided on his or her inward journey to the self and to the Self, God within, a process at once of individuation and of sanctification. Wholeness, the only viable holiness of life, as measured by the degree of interior integration and raised consciousness both in sensitivity to other human beings and in response to the love of God, is the never fully realized objective. Now, of course, in this quest problems, even road blocks, are encountered and the principles of Jungian psychology are applied in dealing with them. It is not merely self-understanding to the end of resolution of conflicts that is involved. There is also need consciously to understand the dynamics within the psyche in terms of the Jungian myth in order to elicit a creative tension between opposing psychic forces. This would make possible a tenable conjunction of opposites, which often constitutes the narrow way into life for the individual. Indeed, maladjustment in some areas rather than adjustment may be the way ahead, in sharp contrast to the usual objective of psychotherapy.

On the other hand, if the guidance is effective or efficacious it will inevitably be therapeutic at many points.

The disabling aspects of conflicts will be overcome and the consequent draining of energies will be reversed. No one is without neuroses, real or incipient, debilitating or in danger of becoming so. It is important to point out that with reference to other forms of therapy, however, spiritual guidance is the all-inclusive process. No aspect of the consultee's life and personality is beyond the interest and purview of the spiritual guide. Dealing with certain physiological and psychological conditions of the consultee may be beyond the competence of the individual spiritual guide. One is well advised to have special training in this crucial form of discernment and to be sufficiently humble to make wise and prompt referral. But the guide is limited in her or his sphere of inquiry and involvement with the consultee by reason of limitations in training and background, not by the nature and domain of the process itself. The consultee is a psychosomatic entity, however ill or fragmented. Every aspect of his or her being and doing is affected by every other aspect.

A spiritual guide of Carl Jung's stature and training in the sciences of medicine and psychology, as well as existential and vicarious religious experience, has a great advantage. Such a person can both perceive and deal with the psychosomatic reality of the consultee on a number of levels simultaneously. Most spiritual guides are more limited, but the limitations extend only as far as their competence in terms of training and ability. The guide may be trained in one or more techniques of psychotherapy, such as psychosynthesis, bioenergetic feedback, psychodrama, gestalt therapy, transactional analysis, music, art or dance therapy. Any one of these approaches might be used effectively when indicated in the course of the guidance, or referral may be made to supportive therapy concurrently. Any therapeutic technique that is authentic and proven sound may be relevant to the condition or growth of a given consultee at a particular time. The spiritual guide is dealing with the whole person, not merely in the space-time contiuum of ongoing life but that life "under the aspect of the eternal."

But isn't this claim presumptuous? Admittedly so! No

vocation is so inherently vulnerable to such monstrous inflation. The shadow of this ministry is horrendous! But to claim for it less than its full potential is to fail to do it justice. Full consciousness of its very awesomeness is the only guarantee of appropriate humility and the only safeguard against its abuse. Malpractice here may well qualify as the unforgiveable sin against the Holy Spirit. The only appropriate posture for the practice of this ministry is one of fear and trembling. To "play God" here, however subtly and unconsciously, is the ultimate blasphemy. On the other hand, humbly to serve as an instrument for the formation of the inner life of another psyche, under God, is to serve, along with the consultee, as co creator with God.

THE PRESENCE OF THE THIRD: THE HOLY SPIRIT

Psychotherapy in its secular practice is one-dimensional. It deals with the client in the context of space and time, as already indicated. It may make effective use of insights emerging from depth-psychology and deal with dreams and fantasies springing from the unconscious. But it does not become spiritual guidance unless and until the therapist is aware of another dimension, of the impingement of the eternal, and remains conscious at all times of the presence of a third, the living God, as transcendent but also immanent in the client, in the therapist, and, in a unique way, between them. What is of crucial importance is the ultimate concern of the therapist, the context within which the therapist sees the relationship to the client, and the objective thereby implied. This mystical or numinous element must be present for psychotherapy to qualify as spiritual guidance.

Consciousness of this element carries with it several implications. The psyche of the client is infinitely precious in the sight of God. Indeed God dwells within the depths of this particular psyche in this utterly unique and never-to-be-repeated way. The journey to the self and the journey to the Self, God, in this person, is one journey and has one destination. Individuation becomes sanctification, even divinization. To assist in this process is the promise of spiritual guidance. What a magnificent paradox is involved! We are at once autonomous selves and mutually dependent cells within one God-body.

Spiritual guidance must now be understood as taking place within the context of continuing creation through evolution, as we have seen. The individual's solitary journey must consciously be brought into alignment with the immense journey of evolution itself, with its axis of complexity-consciousness. The movement of the immense journey is toward higher consciousness and more profound amorization, involving ever more extraordinary integration or wholeness because of the ever greater complexity of the human psychosomatic union.

Spiritual guidance is guidance under the direction of the Holy Spirit or love of God. It enables the counselee to discern the presence and the operation of God's love in his or her life. This constitutes the golden thread of continuity from one's birth until now. The counselee begins to experience this unrequited love of God in the depths of his or her own being. We recall the lines quoted earlier from Robert Frost:

> Once to have known it, nothing else will do.
> All our days are passed awaiting its return.

"Nothing else will do"! But we need not spend our days awaiting its return. "Once to have known it" is quite enough. It never abandons us. Moreover, it returns as often as we respond in love and allow this love to flow through us to others. Spiritual guidance involves an evoking of memories of the individual instances of our visitation by this love as a recognition that "we love because he first loved us" (I John 4:19). It also involves an identification of the impediments to the operation of this love in us. Rejection of this love is rejection of the Holy Spirit who is love.

What makes spiritual guidance Christian as distinct from spiritual guidance of other kinds is the acceptance of Jesus of Nazareth as the prototype and paradigm of this love in his relationship to his disciples. It is not that a particular theology or Christology is required. There are wide variations of belief within the Christian spectrum. It is rather to hold every other human manifestation of love under the plumbline of this supreme manifestation: "Greater love hath no man than this, that a man lay down his life for his friends" (John 15:13). It is to see the operation of the love of the Holy Spirit as revealed primarily and fully in the life of Jesus of Nazareth, and to respond affirmatively to his admonition: "This is my commandment, that you love one another as I have loved you" (John 15:12).

Christian spiritual guidance in its contemporary form may make use of Jungian insights in helping consultees to realize higher forms of consciousness, including the conscious integration of the contents of the unconscious in their individual journeys, within the context of the immense journey as defined by Teilhard's myth of cosmogenesis. At the same time, it must enable them to realize more profound amorization or ways of responding to and channeling the love of God on their individual journeys. It may make use of various forms of psychotherapy in the process to facilitate this inward journey and remove road blocks. But these temporal victories must always be seen within the context of the eternal. It must never be forgotten that the real spiritual guide is the Holy Spirit.

This union of the Christian tradition and Jungian psychology must take place within the context of a larger myth, an ultimate view of the universe. G. K. Chesterton once counseled a person seeking a furnished apartment: "Do not inquire of the landlady concerning the cleanliness of the linen, nor the durability of the furniture. Inquire rather concerning her ultimate view of the universe." If this were important with reference to one's landlady, how much more so with reference to one's spiritual guide! The concept of spiritual guidance must be expanded to embrace a clearly articulated ultimate view of the universe. The all-inclusive myth is that of a cosmogenesis as articulated by Teilhard de Chardin, a universe still being born under the continuing creativity of the Judaeo-Christian God.

THE NEW PRACTICE OF SPIRITUAL GUIDANCE
IN THIS CONTEXT

Spiritual direction must now be seen against this panoramic backdrop. It is well now to designate this work "guidance" rather than "direction", for the latter has an authoritarian ring which is inappropriate in our time. We are more aware than our predecessors of the besetting temptations that accompany all forms of "direction" in the shape of hubris and inflation. A new humility is demanded in the presence of the expanding dimensions of complexity of which we have become aware. How can anyone presume to name and claim this gift (calling, vocation) within the awesome framework in which its exercise must now be placed? It is daunting enough to consider oneself as in any sense, however remotely, standing in the great apostolic succession of curés of souls. But in the context of the human condition as it has been revealed in evolutionary and depth psychological perspectives, who can presume to offer spiritual guidance to another? Lord, who may stand? The ultimate pride is spiritual pride! As we have stated, no inflation is more monstrous, no sin more mortal.

Yet, there it is, this calling, rising up out of the pages of the New Testament and laying its hand inexorably upon us. Paul is the first to name and claim this gift for a Christian ministry. He refers to "those who have gifts of healing, or ability to help others or power to guide them" (I Cor. 12:28). Despite the inherent temptations, if the call is genuine, we evade it on peril to our immortal souls. As well imagine Isaiah rejecting the burning coals as ourselves denying the inescapable commission from on high. Of course, this is a matter of discernment. One's own discernment must be confirmed by the discernment of others who know us and are competent judges by reason of effective practice of this vocation over a long period of time.

Mistakes of discernment can be made and will be made. One may also have the gift and become disobedient in its practice. One may become guilty of malpractice in this as well as in medical forms of healing. One must embark upon this vocation in fear and trembling. One dare not enter it if one can possibly stay out, but if the divine injunction is laid upon one how may one decline? The call emerges from the unconscious as in a dream the child, Samuel, heard his own name spoken. Refusal to respond would be a sin against one's own potential being as well as the Holy Spirit who issues the call. If the impression, oft repeated until eventually confirmed in solitude, persists, "for this was I born," one had better yield! The alternative is to reject the one great chance to become, to grow into oneself, and to become instrumental in that vital pursuit for others.

Now suppose that the gift has been rightly discerned. Then it must be exercised, as the night follows the day. It has been said, "a good counselor does not want for clients." How much more a born spiritual guide! Simone Weil knew the tragedy in the paucity that exists: "One may perchance discover a good confessor once or twice in a lifetime." Spiritual counselors are born, not made. There is no way of imparting the gift. Like a musical talent, it is either there or not there. Many in history and in our contemporary world practice this gift without formal training of any kind, as many great musicians have developed their own gift without accredited schooling. The point is that while the art cannot be taught, nor the gift imparted, it is possible to cultivate the gift when it is there. And "the fields are ripe for the harvest," that is, the world is awaiting the advent of more spiritual guides. The Church itself is languishing for the performance of this ministry. Few clergy are equipped to engage in it. Precious few laypeople are authorized or encouraged to practice it under the auspices of their parish churches.

A PROGRAM OF CULTIVATION

Then how does one go about devising an adequate program of cultivation? Of course it would be desirable if every guide could have a full theological education and be the recipient of a Jungian analysis or its equivalent. But this would unnecessarily limit the field of prospective guides. Moreover, such exclusivism would violate the central principle that this is a form of ministry equally open to the laity and of equal value to the ordained ministry.

The only sound continuing education for this awesome vocation is a disciplined, lifelong inward journey. The deepest qualification is becoming increasingly a contemplative. The sustained cultivation of what St. Paul called "the life that is hid with Christ in God" (Col. 3:3) constitutes the never-ending training. Everyone has the mystical faculty by virtue of being human. But it behooves the would-be spiritual guide to dedicate himself or herself especially to the cultivation of the mystical faculty. Among other things, this involves a sustained exposure to the cultivated mystics. Robert Hutchens felt that all sound education was exposure to greatness. Even more is this true when continuing education for spiritual guidance is involved. Other disciplines that would qualify as constants are prayer in the classic forms of meditation (praise, confession, thanksgiving, intercession and petition), contemplation or the prayer of quiet and adoration, some regular form of fasting, reflection with creative imagination upon the Scriptures, keeping a journal in which to record dreams and fantasies as a discipline of communication with God in the unconscious. To this should be added a sustained study of the psychology of C. G. Jung, and if possible some Jungian counseling, if not analysis.

The central idea in the continuing cultivation of the talent is that of being "on journey". No one can presume to accompany, much less guide another unless he or she has been over a period of years on a profound inward journey to the self (individuation) and to the Self or God within (sanctification). Any program of study must contribute in some effective way to making this inward journey more authentic and more effective with the vocation in mind. Clearly such a study must include an understanding of the heritage of Christian spiritual direction and its historical practitioners. This study must be informed and reformed by a thorough grasp of Jung's myth of the psyche and

Teilhard's myth of cosmogenesis. The elements of mystical religion and their applicability must be understood and experienced. Some acquaintance with Ira Progoff's intensive journal would seem indicated. The use of the Bible for human transformation would ground our practice where our roots still lie. Some review of both the constants and variables in a disciplined life in the Spirit is essential.

Probably any adequate program of cultivation should extend over a two-year period on a part-time basis. It would be of value if the meetings of the participants could take place for a twenty-four hour period. The residency aspect is important. In each of the twenty-four hour periods there could be three seminars of two hours each, a processing session, small group sharing, worship periods, meals and overnight together. In the second year, there should be periods of sharing experiences in the practice of spiritual guidance as well as sharing of inward journeys.

In this way there would develop a deep bondedness between the participants. The quality of meeting through such an intensive program would be deep-level. Inevitably, individual and corporate shadows would be evoked. Members of the group would learn much about themselves in these encounters, and the sacrament of forgiveness and reconciliation would not be far to seek. One of the by-products of the experience would be the salutary effect of the leveling process with regard to clerical and lay status. Though the clergy and theological students would generally bring more acquaintance with the study of Scripture and theology, the approach to these disciplines would be such that there would be no appreciable difference in the validity and authenticity of the insights shared by clergy and laity.

The program by reason of limitation of time and energy could not match the training in counseling techniques offered by secular programs. The training would mainly have to do with the inward journey in the context of historical Christian spiritual direction and some grasp of Jungian psychology. The seminars would be concerned with deepening this journey that one may qualify to accompany another on his or her journey. The participants should have been engaged for some years on such a journey, have known something of the mid-life crisis, have assimilated some measure of interior suffering, and identified some of their own shadow manifestations.

HOW WILL GUIDANCE BE PRACTICED?

How will the individual practice this calling? Each will pursue it in an utterly unique way according to the kind and quality of his or her native gifts, as well as training and experience. Ideally referrals would come through some active participation in a branch of the Church or an affiliated organization. What we are advocating is not only rooted and grounded in a long historical process, but is now informed by fresh revelation concerning the psyche, and can now constitute a "peduncle", the tender shoot of a new, organic movement with capacity to witness to the coming great Church. I do not envision a burgeoning movement to be measured in numbers or power, but a small movement with that kind of authenticity and commitment that can evoke and quicken the latent spirituality of other individuals in the Church, summoning them to their own inward journey to self and to God. Perhaps the Church can come to recognize and encourage such a quiet, unassuming movement and acknowledge the validity of such a lay and clerical ministry. There are indications that this is already happening. Witness the new programs for training in spiritual guidance: Shalem, Pecos, the Methodist program in spiritual formation, Order of the Holy Cross, Jesuit programs, the Institute on Spirituality at General Theological Seminary, and the Guild for Spiritual Guidance at Wainwright House in Rye, New York.

No one should expect to earn a livelihood in such a ministry. All should have other sources of income and practice other forms of vocation. Some will engage in this vocation in informal ways related to their main means of livelihood and perhaps without any compensation, but on a disciplined basis with regard to time and sustained relationship with those accompanied or led on their journey. Others will be authorized by their own congregations to practice this ministry on an ongoing basis for which they will receive some appropriate compensation, either directly or indirectly, through the Church. Those they are serving may make a contribution to the Church in lieu of an established fee, for instance. I believe that in this as in other forms of ministry the laborer is entitled to some compensation even when the labor is one of love, as we trust this will be.

This vocation is not a profession in the usual sense, nor is it a work for which the state can offer accreditation through established standards of training and the passing of examinations. If what is offered is spiritual guidance, it lies outside the province of state supervision. But we trust the practice of this vocation will be disciplined, that those pursuing it will inculcate high standards and continue to encourage and cultivate the inner growth of the individual "journeywoman" and "journeyman" as a contemplative.

Each individual will practice the vocation in an utterly unique way. There will be no recognized, established techniques, but the practice of the vocation will involve the evoking of gifts, a mutual discernment of the way forward on the inward journey through the identification and removal of roadblocks, and the practice of the constants and the appropriate variables in the devotional life to be considered in the next chapter. Nothing, of course, is foreign to the life of the Spirit. But the guide will learn the wisdom of referral to other healing agents when a particular psychological problem lies outside the scope of one's training and experience. What is being practiced in the pursuit of this vocation is an art, not a science: the gentle art of spiritual guidance. It is perhaps the greatest art form of all, as we have claimed, because it involves relating to another "in the things that are eternal", as Thomas Kelly would have described it.

The man or woman in orders who is drawn to this extension of his or her ministry will welcome an opportunity for continuing education for this purpose, even if one already has a theological degree and perhaps even a Jungian analysis. He or she will further welcome the rare opportunity to meet as equals with the laity and share a common ministry of no less value than the dual ministry of word and sacrament which ordination conferred the right to practice. It is hoped that increasing numbers who possess this God-given talent will be drawn to put it to work in a disciplined way in a parochial setting to the general enrichment of the Church.

The greatest qualification for the effective practice of spiritual guidance, from the Anchorite Fathers through the great succession of contemplatives and curés of souls, is to be a lover of souls. This comes about only through the direct mystical experience of being loved by God without reservation or restriction, our recurring theme. This constitutes the ordination from on high. The immediate and compelling response is falling in love with the source of this love, and the passionate desire to be a channel for the expression of the love of God for other living souls. The end of that cycle of love, so set in motion, is not yet. The primary work of the spiritual guide is to find and love God in those one serves, to the end that these may know they are loved by God and are therefore lovable. This provides the only sustained motivation for the arduous pursuit of individuation, commitment to the life that is hid with Christ in God.

Anyone who would presume to practice this vocation must also have a spiritual guide of one's own. No one may climb this steep ascent without being tethered to another to whom regular confession is made and with whom accountability is practiced. Thomas Merton had his own spiritual director and served his Abbot in this capacity. In addition, a guide will need to be bound to others in an ongoing group for mutual support in retaining the original commitment and pursuing the never-ending continuing education in the mystical heritage, Jungian psychology, and the Teilhardian vision.

CHAPTER 6

DISCIPLINES OF DEVOTION FOR THE SPIRITUAL GUIDE

The disciplines of devotion for the spiritual guide will vary considerably with the individual. But there are certain constants which all guides would do well to accept as part of a way of life that has proven itself for centuries with the apostolic succession of curés of souls. Beyond these are the variables which are dependent upon psychological type (in the Jungian classification), taste, culture, and temperament.

I have resisted the temptation to speak of the "devotional life" of the guide because it might be taken to suggest a self-contained, separate part of the total life. The whole life of the guide should be directed toward becoming a life of devotion. This is the reason for speaking of disciplines of devotion. Here again, I must qualify and explain. The word discipline can connote a kind of self-flaggelation which would in the long run be counter-productive. In making use of the word here I do not want to suggest a hairshirt austerity and asceticism. Of course there needs to be a strong resolution to keep the accepted practices and a will to stand firm when the mind plays its tricks of rationalizing to dissuade us from pursuing our appointed rule. But the purpose of the voluntarily accepted disciplines, it must be remembered, is to set us free, to give us wings, not to bind us, however much it feels that way on occasion.

If we are to join this company of devoted souls, we must be prepared to follow in their train, that is, to have the humility to learn from the great masters so that we may become adequate journeywomen and journeymen. It has been said that the disciple is not above the master. What, with unceasing experimentation, trial and error, over centuries of time has proven salutary for the life of devotion for these men and women cannot be lightly laid aside. The burden of proof would rest with us. There are, of course, many manuals of prayer and devotion. The Church in her wisdom has never adopted as standard any one of them. We should become familiar with some of the classics and be open to learning from all of them. One thinks of St. Ignatius, A. Poulain's *The Graces of Interior Prayer*, P. T. Forsythe's *The Soul of Prayer*, E. Herman's *Creative Prayer*. I myself am very fond of *The Guide to True Peace*, compiled from the writings of Madame Guyon, Fénelon, and Molinos, all of the seventeenth century. But none of these is sacrosanct. In the end, having garnered what one could from any of the classic sources, one must create one's own pattern while following the well-charted way.

A TIME AND PLACE APART

While a sustained practice of the Presence is the interior posture devoutly to be sought, it cannot be attained except by extending into the rest of life an attentive attitude developed by disciplined effort in a time taken apart daily. This is the first and perhaps most difficult aspect of the life of devotion. The reasons for this are complex. We could list among them lethargy, preoccupation, a carry-over of the false value related to the Protestant work ethic that busyness is commendable in itself, the memory that the quiet time has sometimes been experienced as boring, fear of falling into the hands of the living God and as a consequence being judged and being required radically to reform one's life. Rationalizing comes swiftly to defense and justifies our neglect "just this one time". But "one time" has a curious way of multiplying itself into many times. Nothing can take the place of this time kept in solitude to focus on the presence of God. Making this a fixed point in an otherwise centerless round of events and streams of consciousness is the first habit to establish, if one would take seriously the need for a gathered life. If one were seeking to establish a human friendship, one would readily recognize the need to see the person as frequently as appropriate, under varying circumstances and in different moods. How then shall we come to know the great Friend apart from setting aside time?

It would seem that this time ought to be of at least half an hour duration if we are to get into and make proper use of it. This should be, on the basis of much testimony, a minimum, to be enlarged as opportunity affords. What time of day shall it be? Most have found the early morning, the first order of the day, to be the best time. In this way it can set the tone for the day. One can move from this center outward carrying within insights and a sense of orientation with which to face the demands of the day. If there are small children in the home or a special set of circumstances or responsibilities this may prove impossible for some individuals. One may find noon a good time, perhaps half of the lunch hour at a neighboring church for those who work in town in an office building five days a week, with a variation appropriate to one's family schedule on weekends. Another may find the period just before retiring most suitable, provided he or she is not habitually afflicted with drowsiness at that hour. It does have the advantage of a kind of unconscious follow-through during sleep afterward, for our dreams are often related to that to which our attention was directed just before sleep. The unconscious, on one level, could be said to be always at prayer insofar as the daimon within it is ceaselessly in motion, quickening images and arousing energy in the quest for wholeness. And we must never forget that God himself has chosen to dwell in this "thick darkness", as was his wont in the imagination of the Old Testament writers. But whatever time we find best for us as individuals, it is important to be faithful in keeping this crucial daily appointment. This is the first and indispensable discipline.

Where shall it be? The setting is of great importance as well. We are profoundly influenced by our environment. There is always going on at the subliminal level a mutual exchange, not unlike a dialogue, which can be negative or positive. If my aesthetic sensibilities have an undeclared war going on with my surroundings at a given moment, I am interiorly distracted and attending very poorly to what I am doing. Therefore loving care must be given to selecting a place, if only a corner in a particular room of the house. It must have appeal, charm, an inviting quality. It must be quiet when I am using it. Cleanliness, order and simplicity are obviously essential. There must be no clutter. A pre-dieu, a cushion if preferred, a comfortable chair (not overstuffed furniture), a book shelf and small table, some attractive floor surface (not necessarily carpeting, perhaps brick or pine boards), a window with textured curtains rather than patterned ones, these suffice for furnishings.

One may wish to have some symbols present which are particularly meaningful, a cross, a chalice and paten, a carefully chosen icon in the form of a stained glass medallion, wood carving or painting — something charged with numinous associations for the individual. Someone I know has some very small, smooth pebbles in a little silver container on his prayer-corner table. I inquired about them and was told, "these are my 'feelies." Serving him as a rosary would for others, he would unconsciously reach for one in meditation or contemplation. The tactile sensation was strangely comforting and "gentling". Many would want a flower or bouquet as often as available. An aquarium for some would be singularly appropriate.

This responsibility to select the imagery and to furnish the corner is something one can only do satisfactorily for one's self. It must conform to one's own taste and creativity and be an utterly individual matter if it is to serve well. If more than one person is to make use of it in a given family situation it must be planned together and any one must be free to eliminate what constitutes a jarring note for that person. The principles involved would seem to be beauty, simplicity, quiet. Jesus chose a mountaintop or garden. We who live more indoors must fashion our own enclosed space that can elicit from us the spirit of worship.

BIBLE MEDITATION

Someday, long hence, the Church may consider extending the Bible to include some inspired works of devotion composed in the centuries that lie between the fixing of the canon and the contemporary world. If we agree that revelation has not ceased, perhaps we should reopen the canon. However this may be, the Old and New Testaments will always have their place of preeminence in our tradition. They reflect evolving insight through many authors across the span of more than a thousand years. In an earlier chapter we noted that the Old Testament represents the gathering of the songs, the stories, the prayers that were fit to nourish the childhood of a Jesus of Nazareth and afford him spiritual guidance. And the New Testament tells the exciting story of the New Israel: the events and the people clustering around the life, the death, and the resurrection of Jesus of Nazareth.

So many have found so much in these writings for so long. They constitute the soil in which our heritage has its roots. If we disengage ourselves from a lively connectedness with our roots in this matrix, we endanger the possibility of a sound and organic growth in ourselves. When we sever ourselves from our roots we become like cut flowers that wither and die. Evolution is characteristically as respectful of where it is coming from as where it is going. Its past is always supporting it. Similarly we must be consciously supported by our past, our spiritual base and point of embarkation, as a Church and as individual Christians, in the Bible. Many in our generation have already become

Biblically illiterate. It is a form of ignorance we cannot afford without great personal loss and, inevitably, stunted growth.

From the point of view of spiritual quality the Bible, we recognize, is not of a piece. There are mountains and peaks of vision and insight and desolate valleys within it, as well as great plains of fertile soil. It is not a book to be read from cover to cover, though this may be done once to some advantage with adequate guidance. It were better, to assure wide coverage, to follow the new lectionary which has become ecumenical in its use and has the advantage of imparting a sense of solidarity with others. There are many good guides to understanding the Bible, none better than the twelve-volume Interpreters' Bible. I recommend working with a competent, up-to-date introduction to the Bible which will enable one to fix in one's mind, in general outline, the historical sequence of the events with which it deals, and the circumstances and conditions to which the prophets spoke.

Then one should become familiar with the personalities and biographical highlights of the authors in the Bible to provide a capacity to visualize what is happening with some degree of historical relevance in a larger framework. One should be able to enter vicariously into the great journey of the Hebrew people from the Exodus out of Egypt to occupation by Rome and to distinguish the various strands of piety and the reasons for variation of emphasis in the New Testament. Beyond this one must learn to select one's own favorite passages in order to return to them again and again for further brooding.

The psalmist offers us a clue for one sound approach to Scripture when he confesses, "I meditate on Thy law day and night." He had no Bible but he had the Pentateuch, the nucleus about which the rest grew by accretion. What the Psalmist meant by meditating on the law of God must have been a kind of sustained, willed relating to the precepts as they impinged upon or spoke to his condition in real life situations and relationships. Were we to do something comparable, it would probably take the form of consciously seeking the Word in the words of the Bible we read daily.

When one approaches whatever passage one is reading in the Bible with a measure of anticipation, it is extraordinary how often the Word leaps out of the passage and addresses us personally with a relevant thought or insight. Those who meditate on the Bible with this kind of expectancy know how often this strange synchronicity takes place. The Word comes through the words to speak to an impending moral decision, vocational choice, need for healing in a relationship. It is curious how varied are the meanings and how relevant the applications of a single passage when it is brought to bear on different conditions and situations at different times.

Jung had an appropriate phrase that may be borrowed for the disciplined practice of meditation on Biblical passages: active imagination. When we bring active imagination and keen anticipation to bear on a given passage we can identify vicariously to the extent of feeling it is happening to us. And in some sense it is. The Bible is not infallible. It is not literally inspired. But it has proven itself a channel for the Holy Spirit. It is a conduit for the Word. One who would serve as a spiritual guide can ill afford not to slake his or her thirst at this well of living water.

READING FROM THE CLASSICS OF DEVOTION

In addition to our roots being implanted deep within the Bible, we have presumed to take our place within a great succession. It behooves us to find among them those individual mystics, men and women, who can speak to our condition. Robert Hutchens once said, as we have observed already, that all real education is exposure in one form or another to greatness. The guide needs to be exposed to the great contemplatives if she or he would aspire to be a contemplative. Deep speaks unto deep; radial communication from the mystic to us takes place from center to center. The Christ life in that mystic quickens the Christ life in us.

Again, the influence of psychological type will be at play here. One whose dominant function matches that of another is likely to speak more effectively to that person. Both are coming from the same place in a sense, and are more likely to resonate to one another. No one can choose with confidence a devotional book for another. One has simply to keep on searching if none seems immediately forthcoming. On the other hand, it is extraordinary how just the right book presents itself at just the right time when one has some inner clarity as to the kind of nourishment that is needed. This is another form that synchronicity takes on the inward journey!

When a proper matching has taken place, and the affinities begin to become apparent, it is remarkable how a figurative friendship builds. Kierkegaard wrote "for that solitary individual". How many (including myself, I confess) after reading Kierkegaard felt with certainty that they were indeed that solitary individual, whether anyone else in the world qualified or not. I am not speaking merely of mutual interests or shared conviction. I am speaking of something that has to do more with the heart than the head. When John Wesley attended a service conducted by the Moravians for the first time he felt his "heart strangely warmed". This is the kind of thing that tells us a particular devotional book is for us. If we carry over from one reading to the next a memory of a particular phrase that caught our fancy and find it humming like a tune in our head, we can be sure contact has been made, we have been touched. Or it may be a strong and mysterious sense of *déjà vu*. "I knew this all along. The writer is saying what I knew was true. It reflects my very own experience but I just didn't know how to say it."

What oft was thought, but ne'er so well expressed.[31]

There is the haunting suspicion that, though long dead, the author somehow knows me, is strangely nearer to the real me than I have been for some time. A bond is formed that is sealed in blood; a soul brother or sister has been recognized.

Such an author may become one's own spiritual guide or guru for a season. One may experience an insatiable appetite to read all the author has written, excitedly going from book to book in hope of happening on one more buried treasure. This may not last for more than a year or two, to be replaced by another, perhaps one who had influenced or been influenced by this author, but a lifelong friend in the Spirit has been established to whom one may return as often as needed. The nourishment continues to be inwardly known even if one has long since ceased to be using this author's writings for devotional reading. To have known anyone "in the things that are eternal" is to have the experience of a relationship transcending time altogether. It has become a resource, an abiding asset to be drawn on as needed.

For example, Augustine, in his *Confessions*, makes me feel that he understands my deepest problems, that he has been there too. His word has therefore the power to comfort and to heal me. I have a companion in my misery who will not abandon me. I might be put off by his erudition, except that he also speaks like a child and with the greatest humility. Above all, since words have a great fascination for me, I sit enthralled before the music of his rhetoric and recognize what an artist he is with words.

Francis of Assisi has charmed me in another way. He appears in *Little Plays of St. Francis,* by Laurence Housman, as a little clown and that quality I find present in the *Little Flowers*. I am transported to the enchanted land of Umbria which Luigi Salvatorelli in *The Life of St. Francis of Assisi* describes in this way:

> Umbria, shut away as it is in the exact centre of Italy, lacks restless and voluptuous brilliance. . . . The entire land is enwrapped and transfigured by a soft, ethereal light. The air of the country is one of sweet austerity, without a touch of hardness or merely seasonal charm, a very breath from the Infinite. The spirit has conquered and is supreme. Of all the parts of Italy Umbria is the nearest to God.[32]

I feel that with the aid of active imagination I can help

Francis in the very act of rebuilding that little church of St. Damian. I do not dismount and embrace the leper. I lack his courage and love. But I identify in my heart with this act of pure abandonment. I see and feel in him not only God's troubador, but also God's cavalier engaged in the consummate grace of divine dalliance.

When I first read Meister Eckhart's sermons, I felt that he was saying exactly what the Church ought to be saying now. It seemed to me the translator put it just right, when he wrote of Eckhart in the introduction:

> He breathed his own endless vitality into the juiceless formulas of orthodox theology with such charm and passion that even the common people heard them gladly.[33]

I liked that he addressed the peasants as well as the "religious", that he believed that everyone, by virtue of being human, is a mystic. "A mystic is not a special kind of person; every person is a special kind of mystic." A certain serenity and imperturbability comes across and a certain salty simplicity, spiced with humor despite his towering intellect. He has been called the "gothic man". There is nobility and even grandeur in his character and in the breadth and range of his philosophic vision. But he did not lose the common touch. He did not "fail to kiss the earth sufficiently". Matthew Fox's new translation and commentary, *Breakthrough: The Creation Spirituality of Meister Eckhart*, a well-named book, suggests how relevant Eckhart has become again when salvation theology is giving way to creation theology in the light of evolutionary perspective. I once asked Richard Gregg what he thought of Eckhart. He smiled broadly and said, "He's a great old boy." I think so too. Certainly the eternal youth in him comes across. There is often a debonair, light-hearted quality that makes the religion he's interpreting seem very attractive. I have always felt that religion like Eckhart's could not only make a person whole but also happy and wholesome company for others as well.

Julian of Norwich appeals to me for some of the same reasons. There is the same healthy-mindedness as in Eckhart. Sin is sin but there is no morbid preoccupation with it. Salvation is not via the negative route of "penance done and penance more to do" but the positive route of claiming and living one's heritage as a child of God in whom God is pleased to dwell. There is a great "bonus" with Julian: she has a contemporary ring, using feminine pronouns for God centuries before the feminist movement. There is not a touch of Pollyanna in her even when she pronounces confidently "all shall be well, and all shall be well, and all manner of thing shall be well." There is something about the down-to-earth, practical, commonsense way Julian goes about everything that makes this pronouncement seem entirely plausible. Not the least of what commends her to us is that, like William Blake, she was both married and a contemplative.

Speaking of William Blake, not only is he both a visual and a literary artist, but standing in Augustine's succession, he astounds us with the "modernity" of his psychological insights As already suggested, both Julian and Blake found in their marriages that union can differentiate and marriage can be a way of sanctity of life. One thinks of another great poet, John of the Cross, and another practical and gifted woman in whom the animus worked for constant creativity, Teresa of Avila, and of the way in which they together illustrate Teilhard's claim that spirituality descends on the dyad, not the monad, though their sublimation of sexual energy enabled them to remain celibate.

To speak of contemporaries that have meant a good deal to me, I should have to include Caryll Houselander, a Roman Catholic laywoman, who wrote *The Reed of God* and other devotional books. Two of her terse epigrammatic statements alone would have held me captive permanently. One:

What happened to Mary is precisely what is to happen to every one of us. The Holy Spirit is to conceive the Christ life in us.[34]

The other:

> You've been told to reverence the empty tomb.
> Don't do that. The Tomb is empty. Christ is risen.
> Rather stand with reverence before some human
> derelict in whom the dead Christ still awaits
> resurrection.[35]

Curious, how metaphors can stab one awake and drive
home profound truths never so clearly seen before,
especially when they reflect mystical consciousness.

Dag Hammarsjkold's *Markings* reveal a profoundly
contemplative life lived miraculously while he served in so
outgoing a post as Secretary-General of the United Nations.
It is rather humanist in tone, but profoundly religious. Also
standing apart from the Church, yet somehow unmistakably
part of the great succession, at least for me, is Loren Eiseley.
His little books of essays, such as *The Immense Journey* and
The Firmament of Time, qualify him as a developed mystic
and serve me as devotional reading. Master of several
disciplines in science, bringing the evolutionary and
ecological perspective to all he surveyed, he thought of
himself primarily as a literary naturalist. It takes such a one,
perhaps, to speak to some aspects of our contemporary need
to discern the "spirituality of the earth". Then, too, I would
add to my list Thomas Kelly because of the little volume,
Testament of Devotion, which became a classic almost at
once, at least for Friends, despite its contemporaneity.

In the last chapter I shall say something about what the
author of the Fourth Gospel and the Epistles of John has
meant to me. But these are a few of my favorites that come
crowding into my mind for acknowledgment. All have
brought me excitement, joy, and confirmation for a season.
Another person's list, no doubt, would be different, though
I trust with some overlap. We have to explore the vast field
and let the books "speak for themselves". Those appointed
to speak to us will identify themselves readily enough. They
but wait patiently to be introduced. But mark this, it
behooves us never to be long without such a companion

with whom we are currently in communion. There is another counsel which I believe to be sound. Though tempted to read on, to unearth the next insight or "bon mot", it is wise to limit ourselves to fifteen minutes of reflection on a very few pages at a time. Finally, do not overlook resources from the other living religions.

MEDITATIVE PRAYER

There is a current confusion in the usage of the words meditation and contemplation, partly due to the influx of movements from the East. In the Christian heritage meditation has always stood for disciplined reflection on Scripture or some religious theme in which the mind was engaged in imaging and discursive reasoning. The same is true of meditative prayer or the prayer of meditation: it is a form of prayer in which the mind is playing an active part. The word contemplation, on the other hand, has been reserved to connote that form of prayer in which the mind is quieted as well as the body. Even images are to be let go of and one is to strive for that degree of emptiness that will allow complete receptivity. Those of the Far Eastern religions, on the other hand, frequently use the term "meditation" where we would use "contemplation". Here we shall follow the classic Christian tradition.

"Prayer is the life blood of the Church." This familiar saying would also suggest a reason for the present state of spiritual anemia within the Church. It is no longer a praying Church. Many of us found refreshing and salutary the public confession of Bishop John Robinson in *Honest to God* that prayer had become unreal to him because he could no longer believe in a God "up there, out there". A few years later he thought to look in the only remaining place, "in here", and he of course found God where the great succession of mystics always knew God dwelt, nearest at hand. God is still up there and out there in transcendence, but only because we first enounter God "in here". When one really believes, however, that God is in the depths of one's own psyche, the sense of what is happening in prayer changes, and the best prayer becomes as P. T. Forsythe described it, "overhearing the converse between the father [or mother] and the son [or daughter] in one's own heart".

Even though we have a new image of the dynamic of meditative prayer once we have a firm conviction of the immanence of God, the five classic forms of prayer remain, it seems to me, essential for a disciplined life of the spirit. A person is still addressed even though that person is conceived as dwelling within as well as beyond. The five forms of converse with this divine person do not change: praise, thanksgiving, confession, intercession and petition. Praise is telling God what we think of him or her. All the great phrases of the Book of Common Prayer and of the Bible are available to us. But just as a parent loves to hear the prattle of this particular child, who is utterly different from every other child in the family, so God wants us to use our own stammering words.

Thanksgiving, provided we are faithful to its practice, can transform our nature into one of far greater sensitivity and humility and perceptiveness. "Yea, a joyful and a pleasant thing it is to give thanks." In our new familiarity with the science of ecology we are becoming aware of the interconnectedness and interpenetration of all things. We have learned to give fervent thanks for much that former generations took for granted: pure air, pure water and earth. We who have seen on television what our emerald sphere looks like from two hundred and fifty thousand miles out know what it means to thank God in a new way for "the good earth". But it is one thing to manage a perfunctory "thank you", quite another to experience the psalmist's accompanying joy.

All of us need to make regular confession to one other human being. But there may be impulses, the springs of evil in our hearts, that we do not know how to articulate to anyone else. These are confessions that can be made only to God. And if we have been helped to recognize the presence in ourselves of autonomous complexes that threaten the integrity of our identity, we especially need to hold these up to the cauterizing gaze of God and ask forgiveness. But it is equally important to accept the forgiveness God offers and to forgive ourselves. Part of this sacrament of reconciliation, as the Church is now pleased to call it, should always involve a self-examination to recollect whom we have not forgiven in our hearts that we may prepare to do so. More than once Jesus intimated that we cannot be forgiven unless we forgive. And there is that wonderful word when the woman of ill-repute scandalized her host because she bathed Jesus' feet with precious ointment: "she loves much because she has been forgiven much" (Luke 7:47).

Questions abound in our minds about proper expectations with regard to prayers of intercession. On the one hand, we are encouraged by our Lord to be importunate. On the other hand, something in us rebels at the thought that the young man whose mother prays for him with the relentless passion of the woman who nagged the judge into submission stands more chance of being healed than the young man, in just as great need, whose mother does not pray. Despite these and many other questions, there can be no doubt but that intercessory prayer *does do something*. At the very least it keeps open channels for the conveyance of God's healing power that might otherwise be closed. And to hold another in the light while entering into that other's shoes, getting under his or her skin with vicarious identification, at the very least does much for the one who prays. When the students of Forbes Robinson tracked to its source the enormous influence this British secondary school teacher had on their lives, they discovered that when he had but half an hour to give to one of them in trouble he not infrequently chose to take the time in solitude, praying with intensity for that one person. We recollect that Jesus prayed all night for Peter.

The prayer of petition which on one ground would appear selfish, being understood as prayer for one's self, from another point of view may be the most important of all. The Lord's prayer gives ample place to it and does not shrink from asking for daily bread. The example seems to justify praying not for the luxuries of life but for the basic necessities for the fulfilled life: health, food and drink, sound education, work, housing, access to good medical care, appropriate scope for the use of one's gifts, the blessing of friendship, and community. But perhaps the deepest prayer of petition is to become increasingly one's self for the love of God. This discovery of identity and the impulse to consecrate it for God's use are sound principles in the prayer of petition. Perhaps the most effective way to implement one's responsibility with regard to this important prayer is to keep a journal with faithfulness. Emily Dickinson said that "identity is a hound that all too readily slips its leash." Keeping a journal is an important way to help keep the wayward hound on leash. It is one of the constants in the life of devotion of which we will speak more.

CONTEMPLATIVE PRAYER

Beyond meditative prayer, but never to take the place of active discourse with God, is the prayer of contemplation. This has also been known as the Prayer of Quiet or of "Silence" and the Prayer of Adoration. Here the body and mind are to be quieted. Proper posture involves keeping the spine erect, whether seated on a chair or in an upright position in lotus fashion on the floor. Sometimes kneeling is called for. Proper breathing from the abdomen is equally important. This involves following one's breath along with the stilling of all thoughts, distractions, preoccupations. Buddhists consider this as a kind of confrontation with "mu", nothingness. Some of our Christian mystics were familiar with the practice, though they would have used different terminology to describe what ultimately defies description. In the Christian heritage it has been called an apophatic (passive) form of prayer as distinct from the kataphatic (active) form in meditation. The ideal is to be as open and passive as possible that God may act, to meet God in the "thick darkness" which is still God's "canopy", and to await there the recognition of the mysterious and ineffable union. Some hold that any individuality, any identity of the self in this union is an illusion. The more constant testimony of the mystics in our tradition would hew to the paradox: "Never was I so much myself, never did I so completely lose myself."

Sometimes the masters have distinguished between infused and acquired contemplation as if one could choose between arriving at the unitive state by certain disciplines or have it bestowed by grace. Again the greater weight of the accumulated testimony is that the prayer of contemplation, when it realizes its objective, is always a gift of grace, an experience of the Holy Spirit praying within us. Contemplation is the desire to offer one's whole being to the One who across aeons of time has given us our being. In the light of the evolutionary context for prayer, contemplation takes on new meaning for us as a conscious attempt to acknowledge the presence of the "within" and to let it come forth as it will. Properly conceived, the inner posture of contemplative prayer is one of "let go, let be" as Eckhart would have seen it. If one is faithful in meditative prayer, sooner or later one is inwardly summoned from the antechamber to the depths of the inner sanctuary. It is a little like letting go into the unconscious. A kind of ultimate trust is required. No one aspiring to be a spiritual guide dare decline to embark on this part of the journey when clearly called.

FASTING

The Bible takes for granted that fasting is one of the constants. We moderns have neglected it. The Catholic Church has released its laity from the centuries-old conformity with a modest gesture of it: refraining from eating meat on Friday. Protestants rarely practice any form of fasting. But more recently from unexpected sources, like holistic medicine, there is coming a new call to experiment with fasting as an integral part of one's lifestyle. When this is disentangled from the vanity associated with some forms of dieting, it appears to have much merit as a means of knowing and respecting one's body and in a real sense communicating with it. We have never ceased to acknowledge that the body is the temple of the Holy Spirit, but we do not sufficiently regard this temple and keep it a fit residence for the royal guest within. We would do well to experiment with that form of fasting that best suits our spiritual need. If we will enter into dialogue with our body patiently and expectantly, a figurative covenant can be reached. It is not merely as a form of penance, recollection, and purification but as a reminder that a great percentage of our human race goes hungry every day that we would practice fasting now as a sacrament of solidarity. I do not see how fasting, in whatever form, can be eliminated from the constants.

JOURNALING

The final constant is journaling. We have already alluded to the importance of journaling as a form of petitionary prayer, our responsibility if we would earnestly pray to become and to remain ourselves. But we need to log our inward journey for other reasons as well. We need to have a sense of flow and movement on this journey, to be sure that we are making progress. We need also to look back over the ground we have covered, to see where we have been in order to orient ourselves once again and to be mindful of what has been congenial to progress and what has not.

It is a way of practicing gentleness toward ourselves, of quickening compassion, and of acquiring the habit of nonviolence toward ourselves. It can help us recognize "that of God" within us over the course of time. We not only perceive the infinite pathos of our struggle to become ourselves but also develop a deeper love for this mysterious entity, the self, in the depths of our being.

We can benefit enormously by attending one or more of the intensive journal workshops that Ira Progoff at Dialogue House has designed, which offer some twenty-two categories for various aspects of rigorous self-examination. Dialogue, a form of active imagination, is encouraged with our archetypes, including inner wisdom, with other persons, dead or alive, in the healing of memories, and so on. The system is extraordinarily ingenious. Dialogue House, not surprisingly, has become progressively more interested in the spiritual or numinous element of the inward journey. I note that a later book is entitled *Process Meditation* and has the subtitle, "A Guide on the Spiritual Journey".

Another reason for having a journal is to record faithfully one's dreams while they are still fresh in memory. Once written in the journal, the record is there and one can watch for recurring images and elements whose very frequency commend them to closer attention. Jung recorded his dreams and, as often as indicated, tried to objectify the images by drawing, painting, or sculpting them. This is the way to begin a meaningful dialogue with the unconscious.

We have reviewed very swiftly these elements that need inclusion in the disclipline of devotion for the spiritual guide. There is no lack of help in voluminous literature on all these themes for any who want to know more. Our purpose here is to bring to attention in our quick survey the elements that should be considered constant.

VARIABLES

According to the psychological type and temperament, talents and training of the individual guide, there are other practices which can be adopted in one's life of devotion. One thinks of disciplined listening to great music for those whom music deeply moves in a mystical way. Spiritual aspiration, an infinite longing for beauty and truth and purity, is awakened in others by reading aloud great poetry. Others, potential nature mystics like Frost or Wordsworth, would do well to plan regular walks in the woods or rolling countryside. We need to be attentive and to record in our journal what seems to awaken the spring of our aspirations and deliberately to plan more scope for those avocational interests for the health and nourishment of our soul.

Some are learning that the faithful practice of some chosen forms of yoga not only tones up the body but also helps to produce a conscious psychosomatic awareness of harmony between body, mind and spirit. We are such amateurs when it comes to praying with the body. Episcopalians got as far as standing for praise, kneeling for prayer and sitting for instruction. But this is very elementary compared with the creative participation of the body in meditation and contemplation as practiced in Eastern religions.

For some an art or a craft can be pursued in such a way that it becomes a discipline of devotion. One has seen a cabinet maker respond to his medium with such tender care that it appears to another at least as an act of devotion. The same can be true of weaving, sculpting, painting. If we have some creative gift and neglect it, we do so at peril to our immortal souls, as Jung suggested. No gift should be allowed to atrophy without the recognition that this puts in jeopardy one's whole psychic health. These considerations may well give us pause and prompt some important reflections with reference to our priorities. The holiness for which the contemporary spiritual guide strives is wholeness of life, calling for a delicate balance of the use of one's talents, the performance of one's responsibilities, and the lively maintenance of relationships so that when one undertakes to guide another, one comes to it as centered and as whole as possible at that moment.

CHAPTER 7

THE DYNAMICS OF THE COUNSELING SESSION

It has been made clear, I trust, that spiritual guidance takes an infinite variety of forms and can be said to be going on much of the time in many occupations and in many unexpected ways, depending on the conscious needs and receptivity of those involved. One could say that life itself is the great spiritual guide if one were only attentive enough to respond. It is also true that our great Mother, the earth, in her own evolving spirituality, has made provision for a vast range of processes that do in effect guide us spiritually to the extent that we have eyes to see and ears to hear. Churches provide worship and prayer services, sharing and study groups. Insofar as secular institutions such as public schools, civic organizations, community art centers, special interest groups, charitable and nonprofit organizations further cultural enrichment, there is also a measure of spiritual guidance involved. We must never forget that growth in the life of the Spirit involves a harmonizing, a bringing into wholeness of every aspect of life, not a specialization and cultivation in one isolated area.

THE INWARD POSTURE OF THE GUIDE

This said, and its truth recognized, we shall now turn to the more specific practice of the gentle art of spiritual guidance in the one-to-one session of an hour or more duration. The first thing we must acknowledge, since we are talking about an art and not a science, is the fact that every artist, in this area as in others, will practice the art in an utterly unique way. That is the nature of art. Science develops by accumulating evidence from individual instances. Once constancy can be established through documentation, science has no further use for the individual instance. It is exactly the opposite with art. One may observe certain universal principles at work, but the object of attention is and remains the solitary instance or creation. Individuality is sanctified. Let an artist, Wordsworth, say it for us:

> . . . there's a tree, of many one,
> A single field which I have looked upon.[36]

Not only will every artist here practice this greatest of the arts in a unique, never-to-be-repeated way, but each artist will practice the art in a way he or she knows to be markedly different with each counselee. This is because each of these individuals with whom one counsels is utterly unique and the art is always performed with reference to this unique person before one. The relationship is one of a kind, calling for a great sensitivity and perception, above all an awareness on the part of the guide of the need to become an instrument of the Holy Spirit and to be used at this moment with this particular counselee in a free, creative, reverent, and utterly individual way. Spontaneity, reverence, and readiness to let go on the part of the guide, willingness to turn it over, as it were, to the Spirit, are essential. As the painter or sculptor submits to the muse who directs the movement of brush or chisel, so the guide submits to the will of the Holy Spirit within. I do not mean that the guide is always literally conscious of this presence of a third orchestrating the music. I am talking rather about the principle involved and the overall understanding of it.

The guide needs to approach the counseling session with the awareness that she or he will be standing on holy ground. This calls for an inner consciousness of the One in whose hands the baton rests when the meeting takes place, and an informed awareness of the need to prepare oneself in advance to enter the sanctuary. One does not just come blundering in like a bull in a china shop. Only the well-trained bull in the Merrill Lynch advertisement can be trusted to trot down the aisle without smashing the fine glassware to the right and left with his menacing horns. No one can rehearse and stage the counseling session in this miraculous way. Moreover the guide must desire to be a dedicated instrument, not just "in general", but for this particular meeting with this particular person. In Buber's sense, it must always be an I-Thou meeting, never an I-it meeting, for the guide and the counselee. Buber says all real life is meeting. And every spiritual guide knows that the quality of the meeting in the session is in truth a life and death matter.

This recognition requires that the guide assume responsibility for holding the counselee periodically in the light in intercessory prayer. Also, and just as important, the guide is to prepare for the particular session with prayer before it begins. Then, after every session, it is helpful if the guide records in a few lines the significant things that happened, the unexpected turn things took, the responsibilities assigned for the interim in terms of action or reflection, the most fruitful themes to pick up next time. This recording will help prepare the guide for the next session, alerting him or her to the recollection of opportunities for further exploration the last session offered. Since it is a journey on which the counselee is embarked, the guide needs to preserve a sense of movement, of some form of progression. Prayer for the counselee, prayer to prepare oneself, and review of the notes from the last session are central in preparation.

Another requirement of the guide is to come to the

session free of preoccupation, unhurried and well rested. Herein lies a critical difference between psychotherapy and spiritual guidance. The therapist with reasonable stamina may effectively see as many as six clients or patients a day, fitted crisply into carefully-measured fifty-minute periods. My own conviction is that a spiritual guide cannot do justice to more than three counselees a day, generously spaced, since the Holy Spirit is no respector of a metronome in this vocation. Indeed the individual session may need to run well over an hour, though the law of diminishing returns is operative here as elsewhere, and a not insignificant part of the art is sensing the right moment to end the counseling session, even if that be early in a given instance. One exception to this might be a Retreat where one may want to see as many as six people for periods of approximately half an hour in order to see everyone personally during the Retreat.

The point we are making is that much depends upon the inward posture of the guide if the individual session is to constitute effective spiritual guidance. The underlying responsibility is that of maintaining an inward posture of reverence for the infinite value of this individual psyche whose health and growth in wholeness the guide seeks to serve, under God, in an intensive way for this brief span of time. It is an awesome responsibility, not to be accepted lightly.

ANSWERING TO THAT OF GOD IN THE COUNSELEE

The reason we are standing on holy ground in this kind of counseling is that there is that of God in this person sitting with one. The wonderful counsel of George Fox, "Go cheerfully over the face of the earth, answering to that of God in everyone," applies especially to spiritual guides. I have always thought it such considered advice. He clearly does not say "speaking to that of God in everyone", which might open the ministry to the likelihood of inflation in presuming that we had a message to give God in this other. The burden is placed on us. One is to *answer* to that of God; and to answer one must have heard God speak to one in and through the other. To be ready to make response to that of God in another demands singular attentiveness. The seventeenth century mystic, Fénelon, advised: "To hear the voice of the voiceless one must be silent before him."

This is a tremendous demand on the guide. But if this art is to be practiced as it should be, there is no way to run away from Fox's counsel, to gloss it over, or to say it is a "well-meant metaphor, not to be taken seriously". Fox meant precisely what he said. One has to find, to identify the presence of God, in this counselee and to hear what is being spoken by that of God through the other. Only then does one make response. If so much is required, Lord, who may stand? Only the stout-hearted guide may persevere in this crucial quest. One looks for and finds the Royal Guest in the other and hears God's Word in a sigh, the appearance of a tear on the cheek, a sudden burst of impulsive weeping that speaks of a mourning for the loss of something that once lived a vital life in the other, an entrusting confession, a shared yearning or aspiration. We are then required to make response, not so much to the person, who of course overhears the response, as to the source of the Word, God.

In some counselees it appears to one at once that God is not far to seek. Usually this is because we are drawn naturally to the person by some manifestation of beauty or charm, a reflection of the numinous, a gathered or centered quality. Sometimes, if we are honest with ourselves, we are repelled by certain mannerisms or personality characteristics. Often we need to ask ourselves what projections we are making, positive or negative, because we are unconsciously reminded of someone else in the past to whom we have been drawn or by whom we have been put off. One must keep on looking when the divine presence is not immediately betrayed by a compelling smile, a chance gesture, an offhand word, in the sure and certain hope of finding the One we know, however concealed or masquerading, lies deep within. In oneself, the Hound of Heaven is always in hot pursuit. When we look for God in another we dare not claim that God is less persistent; that of God awaits our search and is as ready to speak as we are to listen.

The response, of course, depends on what is heard to be spoken. The curious thing is that once we really hear what is spoken we are given to know how to answer. The answer comes from God within us. But until one hears this unmistakable voice there is no "meeting", no engagement that can pass plausibly by the name of spiritual guidance. And unless one does hear this voice rather early in a series of encounters, however muted, one had best modestly accept defeat and make referral to another spiritual guide. Dean Willard Sperry in a little book entitled *The Two Must Face a Third*, once maintained that no love relationship between man and woman could long remain creative in which the two did not face in some sense a third, whether this be a shared commitment to a cause, a child of their bearing, or a sense of God's presence in the relationship. Certainly no relationship between guide and counselee can come into being, much less survive, apart from this consciousness on the part of the guide.

THE TRANSFERENCE

One of the responsibilities of the guide is to impart to the counselee a lively sense of the presence of the Third, "in between" as Buber would say, and within both, as the Christian mystic would say. Both "amongst you" and "within you". It is upon this early understanding, constantly renewed, that the safeguard against any crippling transference rests. Freud is quite right: no real therapy can take place unless transference happens. The transference, love for and dependence on the therapist and guide, is the leverage for expectation and hope of transformation or, in the classic Christian sense, formation. But from the beginning the guide must make clear that the basis of a later transference from the guide to the "guide within" is already present. The initial transference to the guide is temporary, no matter how long it needs to be maintained.

If transference is necessary and to be expected, so also is some measure of counter-transference. The guide needs to be drawn to something in the counselee. Here is where inner clarity on the part of the guide is of the utmost importance. One must be surefooted in a terrain which would otherwise become a morass. When one is attempting to pull another out of a depression, for example, one cannot afford to fall into it oneself. One has to retain leverage, keeping one foot on terra firma, in order to help lift the other out of the "slough of despond".

The guide, while conceiving a real love for the counselee, must not become dependent on him or her. There must always be preserved a measure of detachment. This is true especially when the guide and the counselee are of different sexes and the guide is in danger of falling in love with the counselee. One can recognize when this is happening, despite rationalizations. There is only one safeguard, holding this love within the love of God so that one is given to know how to sublimate it. If one does not sufficiently identify with the counselee, one cannot help. Neither can one help if one over-identifies. Controlled identification is the effective course. If the guide does fall in love with the counselee and cannot extricate him or herself, it is wise to forego the role of spiritual guide with this particular individual since one has in effect disqualified oneself from effectively serving in this way. In this regard it is a high risk vocation. The spiritual guide who is either secure in a fulfilling relationship or celibate by convincement is probably best able to meet the risk.

THE COUNSELING ROOM

In the last chapter we talked about the importance of aesthetic considerations in arranging a corner for our daily quiet time. The same care must be taken with regard to the room in which one does one's counseling. Happy the person who can keep the same room set aside for these two purposes, since the same values are to be observed in both: simplicity, beauty, order, cleanliness. We are very susceptible to our surroundings, even when we are not aware of it. An ordered and quiet room can have a centering effect upon those sitting in it. It is quite extraordinary how much it can minister to us. We have spoken of the value of placing in the room art objects or symbols. Simplicity for the sake of focus and centering is essential. If there is a desk, and there probably should be, it should be one where creative work, not business or office work, is undertaken. This makes it possible to keep it uncluttered. Of course it goes without saying that one never sits behind the desk when counseling, but rather with the counselee. The two chairs should be of a kind so as to suggest equality, for there is always the unspoken principle of equality before God, the invisible Third. The distance between the chairs is worthy of consideration — not so near as to be uncomfortable, nor so far apart as to suggest distance and inhibit communication.

It is helpful if the two chairs do not directly, rigidly, face each other but are at an angle, as if there were indeed a third person present. The focus may be on some object of legitimate, not forced, attention. This could well be a fireplace. I have found it enormously helpful to counsel before a fire when this is possible. Fire is a potent symbol: warmth, light, passion, Holy Spirit. Though there should be, of course, a great deal of eye contact during the session, for apart from words this is the primary means of communication, it is a good alternation and source of relaxation to be able to look away from one another. It can even be a matter of kindness and courtesy at given moments of embarrassment for the counselee. One recollects the high chivalry of Jesus in turning away and reaching down to write something in the sand when the woman taken in adultery was suffering under the relentless gaze of others who meant her ill. Furthermore, tending a fire provides the guide an opportunity to rise, affording a physical relief, and perhaps a chance to punctuate something before going on to the next concern. Fire-laying and tending is itself an art, as Jung well knew. He made of it a ritual ceremony — not worshipping the fire, but its God. Carefully laying a fire in advance of the counseling session can be a gesture of respect, even reverence, for the psyche of another.

In those sessions when no fire is possible even when the hearth is ready, some other alternate focus of attention may be possible. I have found a lovely view equally helpful. If it can be a rolling countryside with a pleasant vista and various points of interest, so much the better. If one of these points of interest can be a body of water, a pond or stream, this is an additional blessing. This symbol of the unconscious may subliminally quicken the cooperation of the unconscious in the discourse. A third possibility proposed earlier with regard to the prayer corner was a well-kept aquarium: water, again, with the addition of visible life in motion. Failing any of these, a simple tapestry or painting or vase of flowers may serve not as a focal point but as something on which the eyes of the counselee may rest. The art work might well be nonrepresentational to allow one to project upon it one's present inner state and thereby be assisted in objectifying it.

All these suggestions may seem inconsequential to some, but long experience has taught me that the whole tone of the encounter can be nourished by care given to matters of this kind. The counseling place does not want to be contrived nor striking in the sense of attention-compelling and distracting. What is desired is a combination that speaks of restfulness, stability, beauty, simplicity.

RETRACING THE GOLDEN THREAD OF CONTINUITY

In an evolving universe, recollection of the evolution of one's own inward journey to date is of first importance. The most significant events are the mystical experiences of the love of God. As we have noted frequently, the counselee may think at first that she or he has had none, but this is almost never the case. They may not be remembered because they were promptly repressed, being thought odd or neurotic. When two curious sociologists appended to an otherwise conventional survey some inquiries as to whether the individual had ever had a mystical experience, seen a bright light, felt a warm glow, or sensed a presence, they were astounded to find that a far greater percentage than they ever imagined gave affirmative answer. Many said they had never told anyone about it until this degree of anonymity provided the opportunity. One said he had told no one, least of all his pastor — a sad commentary on the Church. Several would not have dreamt of telling their spouses.

In this "positivist" age we have been conditioned against belief in our richest experiences. They need to be dredged up from the unconscious in the safe and secure atmosphere that can be created in the counseling relationship. In what Rufus Jones called "the double search" these experiences represent God's overtures to us. We need to recollect and cherish them for they are more important than anything else that has ever happened to us. Indeed, we need to set them in careful sequence and see them as points of contact with ultimate reality. Far from dismissing them as unimportant, we are deliberately to recollect them and see them as points of departure for our crucial inward journey. They give us our "bearings", like buoys or lighthouses at sea. One of the first things a guide must do is help the counselee recover the memory of these visitations, to place ultimate confidence in them, and to infer direction from them for the future.

Of next importance are dreams and fantasies, the ones that have etched themselves into our memories, proclaiming their own importance. At the outset in his autobiography, *Memories, Dreams, Reflections*, Jung says in effect, "If you want to know who I am, it won't do to tell you the places I've been, the people I've known, the things I've done — I shall have to tell you my dreams and fantasies." And he proceeds to attach primary importance to these throughout the book. The counselee is to be encouraged to recollect his or her earliest dreams and fantasies and to remember the "big ones" or the recurring ones thereafter. The keeping of a journal facilitates the study and exploration of these dreams and fantasies. They can often contain the voice of God. Part of the responsibility of spiritual guidance is the discernment of this still small voice in the accompanying clamor of unruly impulses.

SUSTAINED OBJECTIVE AND SPONTANEITY

After the first few sessions there begin to emerge certain deep-lying problems, besetting temptations, impending decisions of vocational direction, difficult or broken relationships, and so on. These tend to build a backlog of agenda items that the guide reviews from notes before each counseling session. It is well to plan an orderly sequence of priorities in coming to terms with these. But it is also important not to be bound by any prearranged agenda, and to remain at all times open to promptings by the Spirit. When there are signs of unusual tension or anxiety, when the red flag of a stray tear is raised, the guide should be prepared for an instant change of plan. No general forward movement can be contemplated until some immediate concern in the mind of the counselee is aired and attended. This again is a matter of discernment on the part of the guide. It is essential in every session to appraise where the counselee really *is* inwardly and to be sensitive enough to draw out what would otherwise remain the counselee's hidden agenda.

Often the counselee is blocked for some reason and unable to take the initiative in bringing up a concern, perhaps fearing embarrassment or rejection, depending on the problem and his or her hunch as to the guide's probable reaction. So the guide must be particularly alert at the outset of the session, looking for signs of a marked change of mood, any disguised agitation or disease. Ever so gently the guide is to ask where the counselee is inwardly, what he or she considers stimulants or barriers to further growth at the moment. Is anything hurting so that it needs to be talked about? Often there will be a sudden burst of tears. Once again, the source and occasion for the tears is to take immediate precedence over all else.

The counselee may apologize for the weeping but is to be reassured and made as comfortable as possible, not in the sense of "there, there", but in the sense that it is not only all right to weep but also may be the most important thing that happens on this given day. The guide always knows that this sudden burst of tears signals that an important lode, for which he or she has been mining for some time, has been exposed. Often these tears are tears of unconscious mourning for some lost aspect of or regard for the self, a nostalgia for a lost innocence, and the sharp and despairing pain evoked runs very deep indeed. One has but to stand by quietly, encourage the outpouring, and await patiently its ebbing, never blocking it.

As one who has witnessed this kind of sobbing grief many, many times, I want to testify that to me it is the most moving and hallowed thing that happens in counseling. One knows in one's self the infinite longing, the poignant betrayal, and the grief that ensues. There is no greater anxiety than the fear of losing by the atrophy of neglect the one chance to be one's self. Nothing brings "that of God" in the other so near to the guide nor so quickens that of God in oneself as the privilege of witnessing another mourn for the loss of self. This is the unmistakable holy ground of which I spoke earlier. One is witnessing the wrestling with an angel, a crucifixion, and a resurrection all at once. No one can deserve so rich a gift of grace. It can only be received with the deepest gratitude.

If tears are revealing of the depths, sometimes laughter may also evoke a sense of the divine presence. When guide and counselee find something excruciatingly funny and laugh together with abandon, a bond is sealed on almost as deep a level. Laurens Van der Post in his biography, *Jung and the Story of Our Time*, tells how a passerby heard Jung's laughter at a Round Table Conference from a great distance away and was irresistibly drawn to see from what human being sprang so magnetic and magnificent a sound. We instinctively distrust someone who never laughs with abandon. It seems strange to me but I have been told that laughter of this kind is inseparably linked with humility and I am prepared to believe it. At any rate there is a time to laugh and a time to cry and this too is a matter of art, a matter of discernment. Jung knew it. Ecclesiastes knew it. Every sound spiritual guide knows it.

THE NEED FOR A PLAN

We have been talking about the importance of spontaneity in the counseling sessions and in the relationship between the guide and the counselee. But there is also the need for the guide to work out with the counselee a plan or a rule which calls for the practice of obedience and strict adherence to the rule. Here impulse calls for governance and spontaneity takes the shape of going the extra mile on the impulse of love.

All "religious" live by a rule of life. The purpose of the rule is not penance or asceticism for its own sake, but "formation" of the individual, a kind of individuation in conformity with a pattern. The universal testimony of monks is that the rule paradoxically bestows a new freedom for spontaneity. One of my vivid personal memories of Thomas Merton was the mark of spontaneity that characterized all he did and was, and this he was wont himself to compare with his earlier bondage within, what the world would have called freedom.

We have made the point that it is unfortunate that the term "religious" has been reserved for monks. We shall use it now in a far larger context. For the moment we shall call the "religious" all who have consciously experienced the love of God and have responded by committing themselves to pursuing the inward journey to the self and to the Self, God within. It is a very appropriate term because its root meaning is "binding into one sheaf", in other words, the motivation in us to "get it all together", to move in the direction of wholeness, individuation, the only viable holiness. So all "religious," including the uncounted numbers of lay "religious," need a rule to follow in the process of their own formation as Christians. It is the spiritual guide's responsibility, when the counselee is desirous of it and ready for it, to help that person design a distinctive rule or plan.

This is to be understood as a kind of three-way covenant between God, the counselee, and the guide. God is the initiator, as was true with the first covenant with Israel. We covenant in this manner because God first covenanted with us. "Behold, O Israel, the Lord thy God is one God, and thou shalt love the Lord thy God with all thy heart, soul, mind, and strength and thy neighbor as thyself." I have often presumed to wish it had been expressed differently, in a sequence that would have reflected better the reality. "Behold, O Israel, the Lord thy God loves thee with all His heart, soul, mind, and strength, and asks thee to love thy neighbor as God loves thee." If it had been put this way, it might have been easier for the children of Israel to comply. Jesus himself made the important adjustment. "This is my commandment, that you love one another as I have loved you" (John 13:34). In connection with love, this makes the command palatable.

So the covenant or the rule is made possible and desirable in response to the experienced love of God. The Church of God in response to her Lord's inner guidance has shaped through the faithful a set of constants for inclusion in principle in this rule, as we have described with reference to the devotional life of the guide. The first is a daily quiet time with meditation on Scripture, prayer (both meditative and contemplative), and devotional reading. How these are to be carried out for this individual counselee, and what creative variables added, is a matter to be worked out by the discernment of the guide and the counselee in cooperation, with the counselee's psychological type, temperament, and gifts in mind.

The variables in the rule are the utterly individual elements, unique for this person. They commend themselves for inclusion, once the gifts of the individual counselee have been identified. The creative and productive employment of these gifts is not only important for the fulfillment of this child of God, but even important for God's fulfillment in this never-to-be-repeated opportunity to be God within this particular human psyche. So the dedication of these gifts for the glory of God is essential if the individual is to grow and if others are to be served through them. How these gifts are to be developed and put to good use must find some provision in the rule. And since our worst temptations are always and inevitably the shadow side of our best gifts, these shadow manifestations are to be identified too, and taken into account in the rule, so that the counselee may be on the alert against recurring temptations.

The body is the temple of the Holy Spirit. Review of the counselee's practices with regard to rest, exercise, eating, drinking and fasting that have proven themselves most salutary through the years will lead to inclusion of these elements in the rule as well. A monastery regulates some of these things for all its residents. The rest of us are on our own here; arrival at inner clarity and the maintenance of good habits are indicated. The rule does not need to be minute in its specifics but the implications should be clear so that the nature of the commitment is understood. We are talking about disciplines, but disciplines designed to provide the psyche a more sustained freedom and more creative spontaneity.

What we have been saying applies also to sexual energy and its expression or sublimation. This is an area so delicate and intimate that any consideration of it in the counseling session would necessarily await a considerable degree of confidence and trust between the counselee and guide. Something requiring such spontaneity for its very nature and life cannot be regulated by any specific rule, of course. Yet it is well for the rule to recognize by implication in some manner this critically important area which Teilhard saw as directly related to spirituality. The values earlier considered as integrally related to evolution itself — differentiation, interiority, and communion — are as relevant here as in all other aspects of the life of the psyche. The rule might well contain some reference to these values.

So much of our lives has to do with relationship. Consideration of the counselee's network of relationships must always be present. This is inclusive of relationships in the past whose impact is still alive in the unconscious for good or ill. Much may need to be done in the way of healing of memories to set the counselee free for more creative present relationships, devoid of unnecessary projections. The rule should recognize the need for regular intercessory prayer on the part of the counselee for close relationships within the family, for colleagues and friends. This is a matter of holding in the light those toward whom one bears special responsibility. And the rule should include praying for one's enemies, not with intent that God change them but with concern to change that in oneself which foments the enmity — projections and one's own selfish needs and demands. Holding such enemies in the light involves discernment of our own need for reform in the relationship if things are to take a new turn and reconciliation is to be realized. The rule should at least be cognizant of this dynamic and suggest practical steps toward its implementation.

This rule, be it understood, is to be worked out between the counselee and the guide and be wholly and enthusiastically acceptable to the counselee before the covenant is sealed. The guide's part in the covenant, aside from having helped to shape it, is to help the counselee to keep it by periodic review, hearing of confession of failure, and reassuring the counselee of the forgiveness of God and of the need to accept forgiveness in a thoroughgoing way. In addition the covenant requires of the guide a personal dedication to serving as faithfully and effectively as possible in this role.

Finally, it is well if the covenant or rule is reviewed from time to time to provide opportunity for change, elimination of some items, modification or addition of others. The counselee also needs to have a theoretical "out" in terms of abandoning the whole idea. This is not unlike the successive stages a novice goes through in a monastery before final and irrevocable vows are taken. The guide and counselee may never wish to come to this degree of finality but prefer a periodic review with the option not only for change but also of withdrawing and terminating the rule. It is well therefore to make this covenant for a specified season or period of time. This procedure eases any accompanying tension and lessens the possibility of debilitating guilt.

Let it never be forgotten that spiritual guidance is an art, not a science. It affords an opportunity for an infinite range of approach even for the individual artist, the guide, in a given instance. On the part of the guide it requires a readiness to grow through the relationship as well as a willingness to assist the other in growth. The compelling commitment on the part of the guide is to grow as a contemplative, in the cultivation of the mystical faculty. This alone will qualify the guide to become a fit instrument in the hands of the Holy Spirit, who is the authentic and ultimate spiritual guide. Only response to the experienced love of God enables adequate love of souls and constitutes the commission from on high to serve as a curé of souls.

CHAPTER 8

JOHN THE APOSTLE AS SPIRITUAL GUIDE

I want to bring this book to a close by presenting the author of the Fourth Gospel and the Epistles of John as a spiritual guide par excellence. He has served me in this capacity for more than thirty years. I have never plumbed the depths of his wisdom nor exhausted the insights he prompts. I have had two or three living spiritual guides but none has had such profound and sustained influence on my life. William Temple called the Fourth Gospel "the profoundest of all writings". Dean Inge designated it "the charter of Christian mysticism". Luther did not hesitate to name it "the chiefest of the gospels". And W. A. Smart has made the claim that "more people have gone to those few pages for strength and comfort in life's hard places, for deep and abiding faith, and for thrilling assurance of the presence of God in their lives, than to any other single writing ever penned."[37] That is spiritual guidance! And the end of John's ministry is not yet. I want to bear my own testimony.

THE BACKGROUND

If we are right in assuming that this author is indeed the Apostle John, as the consensus of scholars is now concluding, or at least the one, as has been suggested by some, who stands behind the gospel as its source and inspiration (though a disciple of his may have penned it), then we must confess that at the beginning John showed no promise at all for this vocation. Only a spiritual guide of the stature of Jesus of Nazareth could have discerned in him this potential. One of the most compelling reasons to identify this author as the apostle, aside from historical arguments and those of form criticism, is that if this is assumed, many otherwise apparently unrelated facts dance into a pattern and make eminent psychological sense. If the apostle is the author or the one who lies behind the message transcribed by another, then the gospel records so extraordinary a transformation of character as to constitute one of the major miracles performed by Jesus.

Consider this young man, brother of James, son of Zebedee, as he is introduced to us in the synoptic gospels. The brothers are nicknamed "Boanerges", "Sons of Thunder", because of their violent tempers. Two vignettes are provided us in the gospel accounts, affording us actually all we need to know to have a rather vivid thumbnail sketch of John. When the disciples are walking with Jesus through Samaria and are not received hospitably, these two brothers make a shocking proposal. "Lord, why don't you just rain down fire from heaven on these inhospitable folk?" One imagines Jesus' response to have been something like, "You haven't been listening to me, have you? You haven't a clue as to the meaning of my message, have you?"

The other incident involves a request made to Jesus. In one of the gospels, the mother of these two young men is reported to have asked, "When you come, at the end of the times, for the banquet, I want you to put one of my sons on your left hand and one on your right hand." Suppose a mother were to make a request of this kind of a teacher at a Parent Teacher's Association meeting — what kind of a woman would she be? Singularly insensitive, I should think. Elsewhere the young men are represented as having made this request for themselves.

Both the violent tempers and overweaning ambitions are neurotic symptoms of internal insecurity, springing from feeling unloved. We can say with confidence that when these young men came to Jesus they were unloved and unloving. We cannot speak for James but we can see what happened to John from his own testimony.

He experienced the love of God for him for the first time by coming to know himself as "the beloved disciple", "the disciple whom Jesus loved". He will not name himself in the account lest he be boasting. But he cannot refrain from acknowledging that feeling loved by Jesus was the heart of his transformation. Not that the other disciples were not loved. Of course they were. It is rather that he is constrained to speak for himself. It is as if he had but one confession to make, one that for those with eyes to see and ears to hear would account for everything: "I was loved." Someone was once asked to what he attributed the good he had done and the love he had expressed in his life. He responded simply, "I had a friend." John bore similar testimony: "I was loved." One translation renders "the disciple whom Jesus loved" in the words "Jesus' favorite". Could Jesus, then, have played favorites among the twelve? It would have been out of character. It does not correspond with all that we are told about him. Yet every good teacher secretly knows that the only one he or she can afford to treat as a favorite is the least favored in the class. The others will accept this. Certainly John qualified at the beginning as the least favored because of his irritating characteristics. Only one capable of loving the unlovable could have performed this miracle of transformation.

Further, the assumption that the author of the Fourth Gospel is the Apostle John would account for the strange affinity between Peter and John. It is as if the big fisherman, probably the most lovable of the twelve, could afford to take this younger brother in the faith under his wing. He was secure enough to take this risk. They are together at the transfiguration. It is through John that Peter puts his question to Jesus at the last supper concerning who is to betray the Lord. They are portrayed as racing to the tomb on Easter morning and the younger John outstripping the older Peter. It is John who is close enough to overhear a private conversation between Jesus and Peter at the beachside breakfast when Jesus queries Peter about his love for him and reminds him that such love imposes responsibilities:

> After breakfast, Jesus said to Simon Peter, 'Simon, son of John, do you love me more than all else?' 'Yes, Lord,' he answered, 'you know that I love you.' 'Then feed my lambs,' he said. A second time he asked, 'Simon, son of John, do you love me?' 'Yes, Lord, you know I love you.' 'Then feed my sheep.' A third time he said, 'Simon, son of John, do you love me?' Peter was hurt that he asked him a third time, 'Do you love me?' 'Lord,' he said, 'You know everything; you know I love you.' Jesus said, 'Feed my sheep.' (John 21:15-17)

It is not surprising that a conversation about love should have fascinated John. It is clear that, because of his experience after coming under the influence of Jesus, love became for him the most numinous and compelling mystery of life.

THE SERVANT IS NOT GREATER THAN THE MASTER

It is only the gospel of John that records the important footwashing incident at the last supper. In John it appears almost more important than the last supper itself. It is an enacted parable, having almost sacramental significance. Indeed, some churches in Christendom have made a regular reenactment of this incident into a sacrament. The reason the event should have so impressed John, when the other evangelists do not even record it, is not far to seek. It spoke to his condition in a peculiar way, and perhaps Jesus intended that it should do so. Had not the request for preeminence in the approaching kingdom come from James and John as well as their mother? So, in a way unforgettable to John, Jesus is saying through this enacted parable, "If anyone would become the greatest, this is the only way: let him become the servant of all." What John records him as saying is:

> 'Do you understand,' he asked, 'what I have done for you? You call me "Master" and "Lord", and rightly so for that is what I am. Then if I, your Lord and Master, have washed your feet, you ought also to wash one another's feet. I have set you an example. You are to do as I have done for you. In very truth I tell you, a servant is not greater than his master, nor a messenger than the one who sent him. If you know this, happy are you if you act upon it.' (John 13:12-17)

This was one of the hard lessons that John had to learn. But now he "knew" it and was in process of "acting" upon it. Excellent counsel for all spiritual guides, relayed to us from Jesus by John! A guide is not to be above the "Master" and "Lord". By a disciplined reflection that "a servant is not greater than his master, nor a messenger than the one who sent him," the guide will avoid the risk of inflation.

It is interesting to note that once again John is particularly alert to how this encounter between Jesus and the disciples is affecting Peter in particular:

> When it was Simon Peter's turn, Peter said to him, 'You, Lord, washing my feet?' Jesus replied, 'You do not understand now what I am doing, but one day you will.' Peter said, 'I will never let you wash my feet.' 'If I do not wash you,' Jesus replied, 'you are not in fellowship with me.' 'Then, Lord,' said Simon Peter, 'not my feet only; wash my hands and head as well.' (John 13:6-9)

Impulsive as ever, Peter is once more rebuked. John cannot resist the temptation to indicate that he has understood the message better than his advocate, Peter. In a similar way the guide must submit to the bathing by the Lord. "A man who has bathed needs not further washing; he is altogether clean" (John 13:10). Perhaps this is the baptism of the twelve by Jesus himself, a baptism in the Spirit. The meaning of the parable is to be appropriated by the disciples. "Then if I, your Lord and Master, have washed your feet, you ought also to wash one another's feet." Members of any guild for spiritual guidance would do well to find a moral equivalent in a contemporary, ritual counterpart as insurance against inflation.

THE GUIDE AND A COMMUNITY OF LOVE

Only in the Fourth Gospel are we taken behind the scenes of the unfolding public drama to experience the intimacy of the *koinonia*. This can be very instructive as well as profoundly moving. We feel that we are in the company of an eyewitness, through the many other vivid details John adds to familiar stories appearing in the other gospels. We also feel that we are actually exposed to and irradiated by the white heat of the dynamics of love as it was experienced by the twelve in Jesus' presence. We have repeatedly insisted that the first and foremost qualification for an aspiring spiritual guide is that she or he should have had one or more mystical experiences (however undramatic) of being loved by a mysterious presence, God. Now we must add to this requirement of some such solitary experience the indispensable need for some ongoing, sustained, corporate experience of the love of God.

This is somehow to be mediated by the Christ within, in a present counterpart of the community established between Jesus and the twelve. One might hope that for every consecrated guide this would take the form of a small group within a parish church or Quaker Meeting. Any particular church is too large for this experience. It must be a small group within a church. For Jesus and the disciples twelve was the optimum number. For any group to be an efficacious channel for the Christ-spirit that was in Jesus, it cannot be too small nor too large by this standard. Happy the person who finds such a small group within the institutional Church! Everyone is under obligation to seek such a group or to help create one.

The bondedness such a group can afford is indispensable. It not only serves as insurance against inflation, as we have already suggested, but also as an incubator for the cultivation of the contemplative faculty, because the members of the group hold one another accountable in the commitment to become a contemplative.

The great paradigm for us is set forth by John in the thirteenth to seventeenth chapters of his Gospel. It is said of Jesus, "He had always loved his own who were in the world, and now he was to show the full extent of his love" (John 13:1). The peculiar nature of Jesus' love for the twelve, the counterpart of Jesus' experience of God's love for him, is clearly set forth in the glimpses that follow of the dynamic of love within the *koinonia*.

At the beginning of this series of discourses, which represent a sustained communion within the community, Jesus says: "I give you a new commandment: love one another; as I have loved you, so you are to love another. If there is this love among you, then all will know that you are my disciples" (John 13:34).

Impetuous Peter, in his aggressive way, asks:

'Lord, where are you going?' Jesus replied, 'Where I am going you cannot follow me now, but one day you will.' Peter said, 'Lord, why cannot I follow you now? I will lay down my life for you.' Jesus answered, 'Will you indeed lay down your life for me? I tell you in very truth, before the cock crows you will have denied me three times.' (John 13:36-38)

There follows perhaps the most consoling passage in all Scripture, upon whose words millions have hung for comfort for two millennia:

> 'Set your troubled hearts at rest. Trust in God always; trust also in me. There are many dwelling places in my Father's house; if it were not so I would have told you; for I am going to prepare a place for you. I shall come again and receive you unto myself, so that where I am there you may be also; and my way there is known to you.' Thomas said, 'Lord, we do not know where you are going, so how can we know the way?' Jesus replied, 'I am the way, I am the truth and I am life: no one comes to the Father but by me.' (John 14:1-6)

One can say that whereas in much of the New Testament we are presented with a religion about Jesus, in the Fourth Gospel we are offered the religion *of* Jesus, Jesus' own religion. It is a mystical religion. If Paul's mysticism was a Christ mysticism, "I, yet not I but Christ in me", Jesus' religion is a God mysticism, "I, yet not I, but God in me".

> 'If you knew me you would know my Father too. From now on you do know him, you have seen him.' Philip said to him, 'Lord, show us the Father and we ask no more!' Jesus answered, 'Have I been all this time with you, Philip, and you still do not know me? Anyone who has seen me has seen the Father. Then how can you say, "Show me the Father?" Do you not believe that I am in the Father, and the Father in me?' (John 14:7-10)

Jesus promises to send the Spirit. This is because the disciples are incapable of perceiving, while Jesus is yet with them, that the same Spirit (the Father) who dwells in him dwells in them also.

> 'If you love me you will obey my commandments, and I will ask the Father, and he will give you another to be your advocate, who will be with you forever — the Spirit of truth. The world cannot

receive him, because the world neither sees him nor knows him.' (John 14:15-17)

Then come the crucial words which reveal that Jesus believes the Spirit, the Word, the Father *already* dwells in the disciples: "but you know him, because he dwells with you and *is in* you" (John 14:17). He goes on to say, "I will not leave you bereft, I am coming back to you. In a little while you will know that I am in my Father and you in me and I in you" (John 14:18-20).

This is the mystical bondedness which the author of the Fourth Gospel experienced among the disciples and Jesus. The spiritual guide, too, must be rooted and grounded in such a group, preferably within one's own parish church, as well as with a little band of guides who are called to the same vocation.

Jesus reaches for other metaphors to describe the relationship within the group. "I am the vine, and you the branches. He who dwells in me, as I dwell in him, bears much fruit; for apart from me you can do nothing." (John 15:5)

THE PROMISE TO SEND THE SPIRIT

Over and over came variations on the great theme. Jesus' commitment is breathtaking:

'If you dwell in me, and my words dwell in you, ask what you will, and you shall have it. This is my Father's glory, that you may bear fruit in plenty and so be my disciples. As the Father has loved me, so have I loved you. Dwell in my love. If you heed my commands, you will dwell in my love, as I have heeded my Father's commands and dwell in his love. I have spoken thus to you, so that my joy may be in you, and your joy complete. This is my commandment: love one another, as I have loved you. There is no greater love than this, that a man

lay down his life for his friends. You are my friends
if you do what I command you.' (John 15:7-14)

The commandment is reiterated over and over again
in these discourses. "Love one another as I have loved you."
Perhaps the children of Israel would have found the great
commandment of God easier to keep had it been given in
this way, as we observed earlier: "Behold, O Israel, the Lord
thy God is one God. He loves thee with all his heart, mind,
soul and strength, and bids thee love one another as He has
loved thee." Jesus' revision of the great commandment is
notable.

Jesus prepares the disciples for the grief they will
experience. But he comforts them with the promise of the
Spirit. Only when he is no longer with them will it dawn
on them that the Spirit that was in him is also in them and
between them, in their midst.

'Nevertheless I tell you the truth. It is for your good
that I am leaving you. If I do not go your advocate
will not come, whereas if I go I will send him to
you.' (John 16:7)

The discourses conclude with the mystical prayer in the
seventeenth chapter. It begins with the word "glorify" and
defines "eternal life":

'Father, the hour has come. Glorify thy Son, that
the Son may glorify thee. For thou hast made him
sovereign over all mankind, to give eternal life to
all whom thou hast given him. This is eternal life:
to know thee who alone art truly God, and Jesus
Christ whom thou hast sent. I have glorified thee
on earth by completing the work which thou gavest
me to do, and now, Father, glorify me in thine own
presence with the glory which I had with thee
before the world began.' (John 17:1-5)

Jesus covets for the disciples the mystical experience
which was his own: the experience of being loved by God,
and of being one with God. This is the experience that is

essential if one is to serve as a spiritual guide. This is the experience into which the supreme guide, Jesus of Nazareth, led the disciples. It is precisely this experience which the guide is to help the counselee recognize and confirm, if the counselee has known it, or to help the counselee attain if he or she has not yet known it. When John came to Jesus he had not known it. From his own experience of being loved by God through Jesus of Nazareth, he was able to recognize and to interpret for us what is the heart of Jesus' ministry and the *raison d'être* for spiritual guidance.

THE GENTLING OF THE SPIRIT

This love of God in Jesus of Nazareth "gentled" John. The transformation of the "son of thunder" into the one who knew himself as "the one whom Jesus loved" was a miracle of spiritual guidance. And this same John became, through his very writings, a spiritual guide to countless thousands. The unbroken authority extends even to this day. John might well have said to Jesus what David said to God: "Thy gentleness hath made me great." Somehow this gentleness permeates the gospel, just as it transformed and permeated the man. It is the gentleness of compassion. It is not for nothing that the apostle has been called "St. John the Divine", for this compassion is a divine attribute. If the love of God can be conveyed through the written word, the gospel has achieved this. This author loves much because he has been forgiven much. He radiates compassion because he was compassionately received by the Master. His words still have the power to "gentle" because he was gentled.

Spiritual guidance is a gentle art, a gentling art. It can be administered only by one who has been profoundly gentled. And it has the strange capacity, when it is authentically practiced, to gentle others. The guide is not likely to be sought out by a more intransigent supplicant than was John, initially. No doubt the story of Jesus' ministry to him in the Fourth Gospel is foreshortened. One suspects that the process of the gentling of John by Jesus was a long and extremely patient one with many apparent setbacks and frustrations for both Jesus and John. But by the time the last supper comes, John is capable of feeling at home leaning on the Master's breast, which suggests an extremely tender, trusting communion between the two. By the time we meet the author of the Fourth Gospel he is an old man, mellowed, well-formed in the life of the Spirit, a great spiritual guide. Let this not blind us to the miraculous transformation.

Before I understood Jesus as primarily a Jewish mystic, I was put off by the portrait in the Fourth Gospel. Jesus seemed arrogant, if not paranoid. "I and the Father are one" (John 10:30). "He that hath seen me hath seen the Father" (John 14:9). "No man cometh to the Father but by me" (John 14:6). It was only when I realized that such words might have been spoken by any profound Christian mystic (indeed many have uttered their equivalent) that I was free to respond to the gentle Jesus this gospel portrays more effectively than any other. "I am the way, I am the truth, and I am life" can be understood to mean simply that the kind of love that Jesus experienced and expressed is to be experienced and expressed by all men and women. When Jesus said, "He who hath seen me hath seen the Father," he was referring to his mystical experience of unity with the Father. He would have accepted that others with a like experience might well say the same thing.

This gentle Jesus, who appears to be more highly "divinized" in the "I am" statements in this gospel than in the synoptic gospels, is also more transparently human in the Fourth Gospel. He weeps at the news of the death of his friend, Lazarus, perhaps out of profound identification with Mary in her bereavement, even though he is apparently aware that he will presently restore Lazarus to life. He cries, "I thirst," the most poignantly human of the words from the cross. He commends his mother to his beloved disciple, the final gesture of love from the cross:

> He said to her, 'Mother, there is your son'; and to the disciple, 'There is your mother,' and from that moment the disciple took her into his home. (John 19:16-17)

Some well-loved intonation or inflection in his voice instantly identified him for Mary Magdalene as he pronounces her name on Easter morning, "Mary". He pleads with Peter to love him (John 21:15-17) as if he had need of Peter's love as well as Peter's service to those whom he loved. This portrait of Jesus in the Fourth Gospel, the portrait "to the life", is predominantly one of a gentle Jesus, but of a gentleness that springs from consummate strength rather than weakness.

From our contemporary perspective we could say that the Jesus of the Fourth Gospel is one who is thoroughly wedded to his anima and seems to have presided over the marriage of the masculine and feminine in the beloved disciple as well. There is in Jesus a striking responsiveness to and "at homeness" with women. Though the disciples are embarrassed by Jesus' air of familiarity with the woman of Samaria at the well, he is very much at ease. He puts at ease the woman taken in adultery and does not condemn her. Clearly, Mary and Martha are among his intimate friends. Jesus remains unmistakably masculine, but it is a masculinity so strong that it can afford to be gentle.

The androgynous Jesus of Dali's "Last Supper" is perhaps the artist's concept of the transcendant and immanent Christ, neither male nor female, the eternal beyond space and time. But the likeness might also depict the earthly Jesus, the spiritual guide, who had achieved an interior harmony between the masculine and feminine, an inner wholeness, a union of opposites, a gentled strength. Though John would not have understood what we are saying, it is my conviction that he learned from Jesus to relate to women, despite the bad beginning with his mother, and to assimilate the feminine in himself.

THE THEME OF LOVE IN THE EPISTLES

The Epistles of John strike the same recurring themes. The spiritual guide speaks:

Dear friends, let us love one another because love is from God. Everyone who loves is a child of God and knows God, for God is love; and his love was disclosed to us in this, that he sent his only son into the world to bring us life. The love I speak of is not our love for God, but the love he showed to us in sending his Son as the remedy for the defilement of our sins. If God thus loved us, dear friends, we in turn are bound to love one another. Though God has never been seen by any man, God himself dwells in us if we love one another; his love is brought to perfection within us. (I John 4:7-13)

The love of which John writes to his counselees is a "tough love". It is tempered in the fire of obedience. It knows nothing of the saccharine sweetness that cannot confront enemies.

My brothers, do not be surprised if the world hates you. We for our part have crossed over from death to life; this we know, because we love our brothers. The man who does not love is still in the realm of death, for everyone who hates his brother is a murderer, and no murderer, as you know, has eternal life within him. It is by this that we know what love is: that Christ laid down his life for us. And we in turn are bound to lay down our lives for our brothers. But if a man has enough to live on, and yet when he sees his brother in need shuts up his heart against him, how can it be said that the divine dwells in him? (I John 3:13-17)

Love demands obedience. We are not just to love, we are to love, according to John, as Jesus loved. This love requires obedience. Jesus understood God's love for him as demanding obedience to God's will. When he commanded his disciples to love one another as he loved them and as God had loved him, it was clear that obedience to the will of God was inherently part of that love. For the "religious" in a monastic order the process of spiritual guidance on the inward journey to God is designated "formation". Being formed in the life of the Spirit involves the faithful keeping of three vows: poverty, chastity, and obedience. The "religious", in one aspect of the discipline of obedience, live by a rule or plan of life in which conformity to a daily practice of prayer, meditation and corporate worship is required. The novices are under the direction of the novice master and all are under the vow of obedience to the superior. The experience of those who submit to this regimen in good faith is that on the whole, despite the rigidity of the rule, it bestows a kind of freedom which is infinitely precious.

It is well to recognize here, as we have in the previous chapter, that we, the lay "religious", in proportion to our genuine desire for growth in the life of the Spirit, have need of and can benefit from a particular plan or rule, designed with our guide to meet our particular needs. This may come only after months of deepening meeting between the guide and counselee, and will include both constants and variables as described in Chapter VI. Acceptance of the rule by the counselee is a free act of the will. Beyond the acceptance it becomes a matter of obedience to one's commitment.

I suggest we read the Epistles of John for the counsel they contain for all those who would go forward in the life of the Spirit. The epistles were written as, and did indeed constitute, spiritual guidance for members of his flock. The anchorhold is the statement, "We love because he loved us first" (I John 4:19). Jesus loved because God loved him first. John learned to love because God first loved him through Jesus. It is the answering love that provides the motivation and the strength to obey. It is the joy of the disciple to do the will of the Master. Jesus demonstrated by his life that it is the joy of the child of God to do the Father's will. Are we not reminded in Scripture: "Who for the joy that was set before him endured the cross" (Hebrews 12:1)? Obedience, even to the cross, is a joy! John is very explicit. Though he is speaking to his own counselees, he is in fact addressing every spiritual guide and counselee today: "To love God is to keep his commands" (I John 5:3). It is as if John were saying: "This is the commandment which was given you from the beginning to be your *rule* of life."

The love of God is not something in which one is

permitted to bask. It is a tough love that exacts service and obedience from those who know themselves to be the recipient.

> We love because he loved us first. But if a man says, 'I love God,' while hating his brother, he is a liar. If he does not love the brother whom he has seen, it cannot be that he loves God whom he has not seen. And indeed this command comes to us from Christ himself; that he who loves God must also love his brother. (I John 4:19-21)

John is not speaking of a vague intention. One may not hate his brother. The penalty is the loss of life eternal; it is to die while one yet lives. "My children, love must not be a matter of words or talk. It must be genuine and show itself in action" (I John 3:18).

Finally, John insists that one who experiences the love of God and would respond in love must, in the nature of things, become a social activist. The love "must show itself in action". The true contemplative is the only sound revolutionary. Such a one does not grow weary in well-doing. The counselee is not really "formed" until he or she has not only experienced the love of God and responded in love, but also has transmuted this love into service "to one of the least of these", Jesus' brethren, the children of God.

Mystical love enables identification, as Paul well knew: "Who is in prison and I am not in prison? Who suffers and I do not suffer?" The individual for whom Jesus' prayer of mystical union has been answered has this extraordinary gift of vicarious identification. The prayer has been fulfilled. And this, despite the unceasing pain, is also an attainment of glory and of eternal life:

> 'The glory which thou gavest me I have given to them, that they may be one, as we are one, I in them and they in me that they may be perfectly one.' (John 17:22-23)

Nor is this unity limited to the Christian community.

All women and men are already one in Christ because the Christ deeply indwells all persons. This is the Holy Spirit, God within. It is a matter of recognizing a unity that already exists and venturing forth in faith and trust to live in it.

It is with awe and reverence that I have shared a little of what my spiritual guide, the Apostle John, has taught me. He has shown me the "glory": how to experience, here and now, "the life eternal". And he has accompanied me, as Virgil and Beatrice accompanied Dante, on my own inward journey to the self and to the Self, God within.

NOTES

1. Angelus Silesius, "In Thine Own Heart," *Masterpieces of Religious Verse* (Harper and Brothers, 1948), p. 148.

2. C. G. Jung, *Memories, Dreams, Reflections* (Vintage Books, Random House, 1965), p. 20.

3. Ibid., pp. 108-109.

4. Pierre Teilhard de Chardin, *The Phenomenon of Man* (Harper and Row, 1961, p. 218.

5. Ibid.

6. Quoted in Henri de Lubac, *Teilhard de Chardin: The Man and His Meaning* (Mentor-Omega Book, New American Library, 1967), p. 132.

7. Pierre Teilhard de Chardin, *The Phenomenon of Man*, p. 233.

8. Pierre Teilhard de Chardin, *The Divine Milieu* (Harper and Row, 1965), p. 46.

9. Pierre Teilhard de Chardin, *The Heart of Matter* (Hercourt Brace Jovanovich, 1979), p. 98.

10. Pierre Teilhard de Chardin, *The Divine Milieu,* p. 104.

11. Soren Kierkegaard, *Purity of Heart* (Harper Torchbooks, Harper and Brothers, 1956), paraphrase of p. 187.

12.   Pierre Teilhard de Chardin, "The Evolution of Chastity" in *Toward the Future* (Harcourt, Brace, Jovanovich, 1975), p. 67.

13.   Remy de Gourmant, *Physique de l'amour* (Paris, 1940), p. 13.

14.   Pierre Burney, *Sketch for a Morality of Love: A Tentative Application of Teilhardian Methods* (Perspectives II), p. 60.

15.   Pierre Teilhard de Chardin, "The Evolution of Chastity" in *Toward the Future*, p. 63.

16.   Ibid., p. 64.

17.   Ibid., p. 65.

18.   Ibid., p. 66.

19.   Ibid., p. 68.

20.   Ibid., p. 69.

21.   Ibid., p. 71.

22.   Ibid., pp. 71-72.

23.   Ibid., p. 81.

24.   Ibid.

25.   Ibid., pp. 85, 86.

26.   Ibid., pp. 86-87.

27.   Jolande Jacobi, *Masks of the Soul* (Eerdmans Publishing Company, 1976), p. 72.

28.   Ibid., p. 70.

29.   Erich Neumann, *Amor and Psyche* (Bollingen Series LIV, Princeton University Press, 1971), pp. 109-110.

30.   Ibid., pp. 85, 90.

31.   Alexander Pope, "Essay on Criticism, Part II," line 97.

32.   Luigi Salvatorelli, *The Life of St. Francis of Assisi* (Alfred Knopf, 1928), pp. 5-6.

33.   Raymond Bernard Blakney, *Meister Eckhart: A Modern Translation* (Harper and Brothers, 1941), p. XXVIII.

34.   Caryll Houselander, *The Reed of God* (Sheed and Ward, 1954), paraphrase of p. 50.

35.   Ibid., paraphrase of p. 160.

36.   William Wordsworth, "Intimations of Immortality from Recollections of Early Childhood," lines 51-52.

37.   W.A. Smart, *The Spiritual Gospel,* Abingdon-Cokesbury 1945, pp. 133-134.